Courage to Begin Again

Also by Ron Lee Davis:

Gold in the Making

A Forgiving God in an Unforgiving World*

The Healing Choice

A Time for Compassion

*published by Harvest House

Courage to Begin Again

Ron Lee Davis

with Jim Denney

HARVEST HOUSE PUBLISHERS
Eugene, Oregon 97402

Some names, places, and events in this book have been altered in order to protect the privacy of the individuals involved.

COURAGE TO BEGIN AGAIN

Copyright © 1988 by Ron Lee Davis
Published by Harvest House Publishers
Eugene, Oregon 97402

Library of Congress Catalog Card Number 87-081662
ISBN 0-89081-607-7

To Elizabeth,
my mother and my friend,
who has always modeled to me
by her life
that our God is One of
relentless, joyful, extravagant love.

About the Authors

Ron Lee Davis is the senior pastor of the 2,000-member Community Presbyterian Church of Danville, California, located 30 miles east of San Francisco. He is in demand as a speaker throughout the United States and has addressed conferences in Asia, Africa, and Europe. He is the author of four other books: *Gold in the Making, A Forgiving God in an Unforgiving World, The Healing Choice,* and *A Time for Compassion.*

James D. Denney, who has served as coauthor on all of Ron Davis's books, is a free-lance writer living in Fresno, California.

Contents

1

A Journey of Discovery

I feel sidetracked, set on a shelf. I look inside myself and find discontentment, confusion—and guilt. A lot of guilt. I feel like such a failure.

If only I could undo the mistakes of the past. If only I could have a new beginning in life.

I know you've felt that way. I have too.

Yet I believe there *can* be a new beginning in your future. I say that with confidence because I've experienced that new beginning myself. In fact, this book has been for me a journal of my own deeper discovery of the God of a new beginning. I hope you will find it not only a journal, but also a *journey* of discovery. And I hope that *together* we can find that new beginning you are seeking.

Let's talk about it.

First, let me share with you a little of my own brokenness—and my own healing. It's an experience from my past that until now I've only talked about with a few intimate friends. It's about the regret and guilt I felt after the death of my father almost 15 years ago. And it's about the new beginning I've received from God.

My dad pastored a Presbyterian church in a little town in Iowa. Throughout his life, Dad enjoyed excellent health. In fact, illness never once kept him out of the pulpit throughout his 35 years of ministry. At 64, he was approaching retirement with vigor and enthusiasm, eagerly looking forward to the increased time he would have for his family, friends, and many hobbies.

A couple of years earlier I had started a singing group called The Children of Hope. We toured the Midwest from our home base—a large Minneapolis church where I was youth pastor. We even made two record albums. Our tours took us to Iowa several times, and we always visited the church where I grew up.

On one tour, our 40-member group was traveling by bus to my home town for another concert. Some of the young people were talking about my dad, saying how they appreciated getting to know him and how they would like to do something special to honor him for his approaching retirement. Their idea was to buy a plaque and surprise him by presenting it at the end of the concert. When they asked me what I thought, I told them he would probably be honored and touched by such a gesture.

The church was packed to the walls the night of the concert. People from all across the community came to hear The Children of Hope share Christ in song and personal testimony. Near the end of the concert, two members of our group stepped forward and asked my dad to come to the platform. There, to Dad's complete surprise, they presented him with the plaque. One of the young people read the inscription, taken from Paul's words in 2 Timothy 4:7: "I have fought a good fight, I have finished my course, I have kept the faith." The personal inscription was also read: "With love to Reverend D.C. Davis, from The Children of Hope."

The entire audience rose to its feet and gave Dad a long, loud ovation. My father was visibly moved. I noted with concern that his hands were quivering and that tears came to his eyes. He was uncertain what to do or say in response. So after standing in front of the applauding audience for several minutes, he just returned to his seat. Clearly, the tribute and the plaque meant a great deal to him, even though the surprise had staggered him even more than I had anticipated.

By the following evening, our group had traveled to the next small town in Iowa. Late that night—only 30 hours after my dad received the plaque—I was awakened by a phone call. I was told that my father had suffered a massive heart attack and had been rushed to the hospital.

I felt as if I'd been punched in the stomach. My dad had always been a stable fixture in my life. But suddenly my "indestructible" dad was in the hospital fighting for his life.

And then the thought occurred to me: *What could have caused his heart attack? Was the surprise last night too much of a shock for him? Am I to blame for bringing this on?* I tried to push these dark thoughts from my mind as a close friend drove me the 50 miles back to my home town. But the nagging feelings of doubt and guilt would not let me go.

For the next three weeks—the final three weeks of my dad's life—I spent as much time as possible in his hospital room. Together Dad and I enjoyed many long talks filled with reminiscence and laughter. For awhile, it seemed he was recovering. The doctors predicted he would soon be able to return home. But at the end of those three weeks, he suffered a second heart attack. My father was suddenly gone.

After the funeral, many people came to the house to express their love. Some of them paused to read the plaque in the living room: "I have fought a good fight, I have finished my course, I have kept the faith." It seemed that so many of them made the same comment: "God's timing is amazing! It's so fitting that God would give Reverend Davis this wonderful honor in the closing days of his life."

But was it really God's timing?

In the months following my father's death, I often struggled with insomnia and guilt feelings. I wondered if I had inadvertently caused the stress that triggered his fatal heart attack. I often asked myself if I could have done something to ease the shock to my dad the night of the concert. Perhaps when the young people suggested surprising him I could have said, "Let's at least tip him off beforehand that we have something special planned." Perhaps if the shock had been eased somehow, he might not have died.

Hoping I was mistaken about the cause of my dad's sudden death, I began to research the causes of heart attacks. In fact the subject became an obsession with me. I read all the articles I could find on heart attacks. I talked to several physicians. What I learned gave me no comfort: happy, positive events can tax the human system as much as stress from unpleasant events.

I will never know for sure what triggered my dad's heart attack. If I had handled things differently, would my dad have lived to enjoy his retirement and his grandchildren? Even today I can only speculate.

After the funeral, I returned to my work. Yet there seemed to be no joy or purpose in what I was doing. I knew it was normal to feel acute grief and depression for a long time after a loss. But it didn't seem at all normal to be haunted by the guilt and sense of responsibility I felt for my father's death. If only I could have changed the past—or just known for sure exactly what triggered my dad's heart attack.

These were the doubts that overshadowed me as I entered the office of a Christian counselor. I had never been to a counselor before. But I realized that I needed special help, a quality of insight I didn't possess in my own wisdom. Thus began many painful hours spent gaining deeper understanding of my feelings about my dad's death. It was a transforming process—but it was an agonizingly *slow* process. There was no sudden breakthrough—just a long journey toward freedom from guilt and a fresh experience of the grace of God.

I remember one early conversation with my counselor. I was talking to him about how all my wonderful memories of Dad had become tinged with cold, grey shades of guilt, and doubt. He listened to me without interrupting. Then there was a long silence as he thought and prayed.

Finally he said, "Ron, you've got some beautiful memories of your dad. But your guilt feelings are clouding those memories. If you don't resolve the guilt, it will rob you of those memories. It will become too painful to think about the good times with your dad. Ron, the only way to heal the hurt of your guilt is to let the grace of God into your life."

"The grace of God," I repeated. I had heard those words all my life. Suddenly they sounded empty and meaningless, without any realistic content.

"By 'grace' I mean the undeserved goodness of God," he continued. "For example, if you failed yesterday, today is a new beginning. If you sinned yesterday, today you have a clean slate. You don't deserve it, but God, by his grace, gives you his good gifts and his extravagant unconditional love."

I nodded bleakly. It all made sense—in my head. But my heart was having a hard time grasping it.

"Let's begin with the doubts you feel," he pressed on. "You say the thing that troubles you most is not knowing. You wonder, 'Did I or didn't I contribute to my father's fatal heart attack?' Let's face the worse possibility. Let's say you did contribute to your dad's death."

I winced inwardly and began to protest.

"Hang in with me, Ron," he said quickly. "I know it's hard. But it's important that you face the worst—confront it head-on—and get it behind you. Just for the moment, accept responsibility for your father's death. Say, 'I could have prevented it.' "

"I—I could have prevented it," I echoed his words hesitantly.

"How well did you know your dad?"

"I told you. He was the most Christlike man I've ever known. There was no one more instrumental in bringing me to Jesus Christ than my dad."

"And how would your dad want you to feel right now?" he pursued.

I didn't even need to think about the answer. "He'd want me to feel forgiven."

"What would he say to you?"

Tears spilled down my cheeks. All I could hear was my own ragged breathing.

"You just told me that your father was your best friend," he prodded gently. "You know him so well, Ron. You know his character, his mind, his heart, his affection for you. I think you know what he would say to you right now if he could."

My counselor was right. I did know. "I can hear him now," I said at last. "He'd say, 'Ron, it's okay. Believe me, everything's okay. No one ever knows how many days the Lord will give him on this earth. But the days God gave me were good days. I had a good life ministering in this little Iowa town. I had the love of your mother, your brother Paul, and you through the years. And I'd be ungrateful if I felt shortchanged in this life. So don't feel bad, Ron. I'm with the Lord now. I'm where I'm supposed to be.'"

It was one small realization, a little light through a small window. But it was a major first step. After that, I actually *felt* my father's forgiveness and affection for me. It was as though he was reaching across the gulf of human mortality, touching me on the shoulder, and smiling that warm smile of his.

I knew what my father would have said to me because I knew him so well. He was a humble, gentle, compassionate man, always ready to extend grace to the guilty, forgiveness to the fallen, love to the unlovely. Whenever people stumbled, he was always ready to lift them up and help them begin again.

More and more light flooded my heart as I continued to work with the Christian psychologist. He helped me see my father's death in terms of blessing rather than tragedy, in terms of God's goodness rather than my guilt. In the years since then, I've seen a number of people die. I realize now that my father's death entailed comparatively little suffering. And my family was blessed with three special weeks to make sure that there was nothing left unsaid or undone toward my dad. Unlike many grieving families I've seen, we have no doubts about whether or not we demonstrated our love to him. Equally important, my dad was able to leave this world without remorse.

My counselor also helped me realize that my feelings of guilt were natural and common to most grief processes. When a loved one dies, there are almost always regrets, painful memories, and words family members wish they had said or hadn't said. *Grief*, I learned, is almost always coupled with *guilt*. And yet so many people choose to go through their grief alone rather than share their feelings with Christian friends or a counselor. Thus they find themselves feeling completely isolated, as if they are the only ones to feel such pain.

After facing the worst of my guilt and, in effect, experiencing my dad's forgiveness, I realized that there was no possible way to have foreseen what happened to Dad. In this life we must simply rely upon the sovereignty and grace of God, knowing that he is in the midst of every event in our lives. Even though we can't explain everything that happens, we know God is in control.

Though there are still times when I find myself haunted by unanswered questions, I know with all my heart that God has transformed my pain into a new beginning. When we make the healing choice to hand our failure to God, he takes it, blesses it, and gives it back to us in a gleaming new form. Our old pain becomes a brand new ministry to others!

God gave me a new beginning when he empowered me to work through my guilt and grief during my mending process. God has transformed my pain into empathy for others who wrestle with guilt and sorrow. When I sit in my counseling room with someone who is weeping over his past, a responsive chord sounds within me. I cannot remain unmoved by the pain of others, as one who has never known pain myself. God sustains us through deep waters so that we might become "wounded healers" for him.

That is why I have chosen to share my woundedness with you. To me, the words I write in this book are not just ink on paper. These words pour from my heart. And I know that there are people reading these words, like you perhaps, who have wounds like mine. You struggle with your own store of pain, your own sense of guilt and failure. I ask God to use these words to connect your heart with mine, and our hearts with his.

This book is a joint effort between you, me, and God. Together we are seeking to discover the new beginning that God wants to create out of the ashes of your pain. Together we *can* find that new beginning. I know we can. I've seen it happen many times before.

I know many people who have discovered God's new beginning for their lives. Each life and each discovery is a different story. These are the stories of some of my friends. As I share them with you, perhaps something in these stories will resonate with your spirit.

So turn the page and let me tell you a story—and another, and another. I believe that you will find parts of your story in at least one of these stories. And I pray you will find something else as well. I pray you will discover, in a deeper way than ever before, the One who gives us the grace and power and courage to begin again—the God of a new beginning.

2

An Invitation to Transformation

Pam was radiant. The light of her inner happiness seemed to illuminate her face, pouring from her smile and her eyes. The effect was like morning sunlight shining through an east window. She appeared ten years younger than her actual age. Best of all, the joy I saw in her was not just a momentary high in an oscillating pattern of moods. Rather, it was a durable and stable aspect of her character. Joy had become an inseparable *part* of her.

Was this the same woman who had once poured out her pain and regret to me in a rush of bitter tears? Was this the same woman who had grieved so deeply over her broken past, and who feared she had no future? Was this the same woman who once saw herself as useless and totally abandoned by God?

Yes, it was the same woman—and yet she was *not* the same. Pam had been *transformed*.

As Pam and I talked together about her new life, I couldn't help but think back on all she had gone through to become the radiant woman she is today. The daughter of harsh, overbearing parents, Pam craved the freedom to live her life as she saw fit, without any restrictions or rules. Like many of her teenaged peers in the late 1960s, she bitterly rebelled against her strict upbringing and ran away from home.

For several years she moved from town to town, experimenting with drugs and engaging in a variety of liaisons with men she only vaguely knew. From her teen years into her early twenties, Pam drifted from communes to encounter groups to skid row shelters.

In 1974, at age 25, Pam had an abortion. It was legal, uncomplicated, and easy to obtain. She was undergoing group "sensitivity training" at the time. Her group encouraged her to attribute any guilt feelings about the abortion to her restrictive upbringing.

During her early thirties, Pam's life took a new direction. A lady from a neighboring apartment befriended Pam and began to talk to her about the joy and purpose for life she had found in her relationship with Jesus Christ. Pam was captivated by her neighbor's love and testimony. One day they prayed together and Pam found peace with God. Within a few weeks, Pam traveled to her home town and made peace with her parents.

But one obstacle still blocked Pam's path to peace with herself: the memory of the unborn child she had aborted nearly a decade earlier. She couldn't escape the painful reality that she had deliberately killed the only child she had ever conceived.

That's when Pam and I first met. She wanted to serve God, but guilt and grief hovered over her like a black cloud, shrouding her from the sunlight of God's love. She grieved over the years she lost to rebellion and aimless wandering. She grieved over the unborn child she never knew. She longed for a second chance at motherhood, but because of her age and lack of marriage prospects, Pam thought it was impossible to ever have children.

Pam and I talked together, prayed together, and even wept

together over her pain. I wondered what words of hope or comfort I could give her. The first thing we did together was to look at her life—not just the past, but the now. I asked her who she was and how she saw herself.

"There's nothing much to say," she began. "I've lived for 30-some-odd years with hardly anything to show for it. I'm not married. I've ruined my only chance to be a mother. I have no skills. I've never accomplished anything. What do I have to offer God? Oh, I know that God loves me unconditionally. I know I don't have to work my way into His love. But I just feel so worthless, so useless!"

It occurred to me that the key to finding God's grace for Pam's life might lie in her longing for motherhood, her love for children. It also turned out to be the key to relieving Pam's guilt and inability to forgive herself. As an irresponsible, free-spirited young woman, Pam had rejected the responsibilities of motherhood by aborting her only child. This was the fact in Pam's life that needed to be confronted and overcome.

Over the months that we met and talked together, I challenged Pam to accept the things about her life that she could not immediately change: her past, her childlessness, and—at least temporarily—her singleness. Then I encouraged her to keep her eyes open for ways to change the things that *could* be changed in her life. Over time, Pam realized that even though she may never have a child of her own to love, there was a previously unexplored world all around her—a world filled with hurting, unloved children. She decided to go back to school and earn a degree in child development. Today she devotes her time to nurturing children in a Christian day-care and enrichment program.

God has given Pam a new life. She lives each day with a spirit of gratitude for the grace and forgiveness she has received from God. She knows now that God never abandoned her. He was alongside her all the way, gently leading her to discover the unique gifts within her, gifts that would enable her to be a special friend to children.

Pam lives with expectancy for today, for tomorrow, and for eternity. "My baby is in heaven now," she told me. "I know I'll get to see her again someday. I'll get another chance in eternity to know my baby, to love her, and to tell her I'm sorry. But right now God has given me hundreds of children to love. Just at the time I thought God was through with me, my *real* life, my *new* life was just beginning!"

God was not through with my friend Pam. He was present with her through her suffering, her struggle, and her search for a new beginning. He was patiently, persistently, and lovingly drawing her to himself. Today Pam is a sweet fragrance of the love and grace of God to everyone she meets.

And Pam's story is not unique. I've seen the beautiful pattern of her life reproduced again and again in the lives of many other people. In fact, it is an old, old pattern that comes straight from the pages of Scripture. For thousands of years, people who have felt used up, burned out, washed up, and defeated have found that God was not through with them. The God of the Bible has always been the God of a new beginning.

The story of Rahab in Joshua 2 and 6 is such a story. Rahab was a prostitute who sold herself at the edge of the city of Jericho—a disreputable woman performing a disreputable service in a disreputable city. When she learned that God had marked Jericho for destruction by the approaching Hebrew army, she switched her allegiance to the side of the Hebrews, aiding the Hebrew spies and placing her trust in the Hebrews' God. Even though her entire life-style had been a capital crime, punishable by stoning according to the Hebrew law, Rahab became an adopted daughter of the Hebrew people after Jericho was destroyed. A woman of sin was transformed into a woman of faith.

"By faith," says Hebrews 11:31, "the prostitute Rahab, because she welcomed the spies, was not killed with those who were disobedient." And James 2:25 says, "Was not even

Rahab the prostitute considered righteous for what she did when she gave lodging to the spies and sent them off in a different direction?" But perhaps the most amazing tribute to Rahab is found in Matthew 1:5, which records that this former prostitute ultimately became part of a royal lineage. For from Rahab were descended *kings*—King David, King Solomon, and even the King of kings, the Lord Jesus Christ.

In 2 Samuel 11 and 12 we find again that the God of the Bible is also the God of a new beginning. There we find the story of King David—a man who had once followed God with all his heart, but who had become arrogant and self-indulgent. At the apex of his success as King of Israel, he had begun to forget God. One night he was walking on his balcony when he saw a woman bathing in a pool below. He watched, he lusted, and then he sent for her and committed adultery with her. Then, to cover his sin, he arranged to have the woman's husband—who was also one of his most loyal and capable army officers—killed on the battlefield. Then he took the woman into his own home as his wife.

But God in his grace was not through with David, even though he was drenched in the guilt of adultery and murder. God, through his prophet Nathan, confronted David with his sin. And David repented in tears, his pride and willfulness now totally broken. And the response of God through the prophet Nathan was one of grace and a new beginning: "The Lord has taken away your sin."

God was able to weave the pain and tangled circumstances that David had created into his own divine plan. A child of destiny was born to David and this woman, a child named Solomon. And this child grew to succeed David as King. Solomon later built the grandest temple ever dedicated to God, and authored some of the most beautiful and powerful books of the Old Testament—Proverbs, Ecclesiastes, and the Song of Songs. After his death, God remembered David with these words in 1 Kings 14:8—"My servant David . . . kept my commands and followed me with all his heart, doing only what was right in my eyes." That is an epitaph for a life that has been touched by the new-beginning grace of God.

This was the same new-beginning grace that touched a moody, impetuous, profane fisherman named Simon and transformed him into *Peter*, a man whose name means "the rock." It was not a name Peter had earned because he had already proved himself rocklike, solid, or strong. Rather, Jesus gave his friend Peter this new name because of what Peter would one day become. Even after Peter received his new name, there were dark days ahead for Peter—days of dishonor, grief, and remorse when Peter would deny Jesus three times. But Jesus knew that Peter would come out of his trial of shame and guilt with a stronger, tested character. So by the new-beginning grace of God, vacillating, defecting, feet-of-clay Simon became *Peter*, the rock upon which Jesus Christ built his church.

This was the same new-beginning grace that touched a violent, arrogant, blaspheming terrorist named Saul. He hated the name of Jesus, and devoted himself to dragging the followers of Jesus out of their homes and churches to be beaten, imprisoned, or stoned. Yet one day, while he was traveling to Damascus to seize and imprison Christians there, the new-beginning grace of God suddenly exploded around Saul in the form of a blinding light and a thundering voice from heaven. He was knocked flat to the ground, assaulted by grace. And Saul went away from there a transformed man—a man with a new beginning and a new name. Saul, this violent persecutor of the early church, became *Paul*, the greatest evangelist and missionary of the early church.

This was the same new-beginning grace that touched a miserable failure named John Mark. As a young man, John Mark had accompanied Paul and Barnabas on Paul's first missionary journey. But for some reason he had washed out. Perhaps the hardships, the dangers, the sparse rations, and the weariness of the road had taken their toll. But whatever the reason, John Mark had deserted Paul and Barnabas during the journey, and returned home to Jerusalem with his tail between his legs.

Sometime later, Paul and Barnabas were preparing for a second missionary journey, and Barnabas suggested they give John Mark another chance. But Paul wouldn't hear of it! Paul was focused on the hard work ahead, and wanted only men of proven character and reliability at his side. But Barnabas seemed to intuitively grasp what 20th century psychologists and management consultants have only recently begun to grasp: those who fail and are given a second chance to work through their failures usually develop the inner strength and character to succeed in the future. So Barnabas gave John Mark the second chance he needed, taking him under his wing and striking out in a new direction as a missionary, while Paul went his own way, accompanied by Silas.

As a result of the belief that Barnabas had in John Mark, this once-miserable failure experienced a complete and miraculous turnaround. John Mark eventually became an important leader in the early church, and the author of that profound and inspired story of the life of Christ, the Gospel of Mark. And one day, even Paul—the man who had once rejected John mark as a quitter and failure—would say of him "Get [John] Mark and bring him with you, because he is helpful to me in my ministry" (2 Timothy 4:11).

God was not through with a failure named John Mark. Nor was he through with Rahab the prostitute. God wasn't through with David the adulterer and murderer. God wasn't through with Peter the defector or Paul the persecutor. God wasn't through with my friend Pam. And God isn't through with you and me. Even if you feel washed up or set aside, the God of a new beginning is with you, ready to transform you by his grace.

God was not through with my friends Tom and Joanna. Both previously divorced, Tom and Joanna committed themselves to each other in marriage. They had learned from their past mistakes and they were going to make *this* marriage work.

But in the weeks after their wedding, they were subjected to unkind criticism, the complications and conflicts of blended families, and the problems of dealing with malicious ex-spouses. Soon these external pressures began to strain their own relationship. Petty bickering escalated into major conflicts between them. The pattern became horrifyingly familiar and a sudden fear gripped them. Was divorce looming in their lives *again*?

As Tom and Joanna shared their story with me, I realized that they had experienced every level of apprehension, anger, depression, and hurt which comes with divorce and remarriage. "I'm just so scared," Joanna confessed. "I can't face the thought of failing at marriage a second time."

"We really love each other," Tom said, holding Joanna's hand in a way that was both tender and tenacious. "We looked to our previous church for support. But all we received was criticism."

"One of the elders in that church said our relationship didn't stand a chance," Joanna said, her voice trembling and her eyes glistening. "He said that being divorced and remarried is nothing more than living in—in adultery."

"It's been hard dealing with the kids—both Joanna's and mine," Tom continued. "We agreed to raise our kids to be strong enough and wise enough to avoid the pitfalls we tripped into. But it's been hard to keep that goal in front of us. It seems that every time we discipline the kids, they start talking about living with their other parent who is more lenient. We love all our kids so much, and we're sure they don't know how much they hurt us with these tactics. But the kids are becoming really hard to deal with."

"*Everything* is becoming hard to deal with," added Joanna with a weary sigh.

We continued to talk together, hurt together, and pray together. And then, over the weeks that followed, I watched them learn to communicate with each other at increasingly deeper and more honest levels of intimacy. In the process, they discovered insights into each other's needs, hopes, and fears that they never knew existed. They learned that children playing parents against each other is a common consequence of divorce, and that there are ways to cope with it. Ultimately, they discovered an underlying core of joy at the center of their life together.

God was not through with my friend Carrie. Married for ten years, a mother of two small boys, and a full-time homemaker, Carrie had a comfortable, settled life. Her husband provided a good living for their family, and their marriage was strong and satisfying. Yet Carrie was one of the millions of people who, as Thoreau once said, "lead lives of quiet desperation."

When Carrie first began to talk with me, it was difficult for her to articulate her pain. Her long silences and deep sighs were more eloquent than her words. "I don't know why I feel so bad," she told me. "I guess it's just that everything is such a mess."

"*What* is such a mess?" I asked her. "Try to be specific."

"My house is a mess—I'm a terrible housekeeper," she said. "And my spiritual life—that's a mess. And *me*—I'm a mess."

"Why do you say that?"

"I don't get anything accomplished. I look around at five o'clock and wonder, 'What have I done with this day?' I feel like I'm lazy and sloppy. I'm 30 pounds overweight and I can't seem to do anything about it. My life is boring and pointless. I feel trapped. I feel like a failure."

"It sounds like the pain you're feeling is centered in your self-image," I suggested.

"*What* self-image?" she retorted, laughing just a little. It was a wounded kind of laugh, and though I smiled back at her, I ached for her as well.

Together we explored the map of Carrie's past for awhile. As a child, she had unsuccessfully sought the affirmation and affection of an inexpressive father. As a result, she grew up feeling unlovely and incompetent. As an adult, her lack of self-confidence kept her from completing tasks. She procrastinated and puttered aimlessly. She snacked and binged to fill the emotional emptiness within her. These self-defeating patterns only served to sink her self-image even lower and perpetuate her pain.

"Sometimes I turn on the TV," she confessed, "and tell myself I just want something to listen to while I do housework. But soon I'm sitting down with a quart of Häagen Dazs and *The Young and the Restless*. And before I realize it, I've wasted another hour in front of the tube and added another pound to my hips." Even when Carrie joked about her problems, I noticed that her eyes glistened with tears and her voice quavered.

As Carrie and I continued to talk, we began to discover some solutions to her problems. Though I made occasional suggestions, it was Carrie who actually came up with the plan for her transformation. "I can see that I need some structure and some discipline in my life," she said. And Carrie became the architect of that structure.

"You could begin the day with a short time of Bible study and prayer," I suggested.

"Early mornings are too hectic, what with making breakfast and getting the family out of the house. But I *could* have devotions right after I get back from taking the kids to school." Then she frowned. "Of course, I'm always kind of tired right then because of breakfast-time 'rush hour.'" Then she brightened. "But I could make it a *relaxing* time—put on some coffee, lay out my Bible and prayer notebook, and just have a time of refreshment with the Lord!"

"Good idea," I encouraged. "It's wise to work with your natural rhythms rather than try to fight them. If 9:15 is a letdown time for you, that's the time to take a coffee break with an open Bible. Then, after you've finished reading and praying, you can take five minutes to list tasks you need to accomplish." I reached into my desk, pulled out my "Things to Do" pad, and peeled off a dozen blank sheets for her. "This will get you started. Write out your plan for the day. When you finish a task, check it off. You'll feel a real sense of accomplishment seeing those check marks add up."

Then I encouraged Carrie to share her struggle with the weekly Bible study group she and her husband attended. I knew the members of their group had agreed to be honest, open, and sensitive to each other, and to pray for each other within the context of affirmation and confidentiality. Though Carrie was reluctant and embarrassed at the thought of disclosing this part of her life to her Christian friends, she finally agreed that she *needed* to be accountable to others for her life-style. She underlined James 5:16 in her Bible and decided to live by these words: "Confess your sins to to each other and pray for each other so that you may be healed." The prayers and encouragement of her Bible study group became an important part of Carrie's new beginning.

After we prayed together, Carrie took her new plan home with every intention of putting it into practice. But during the first week, her old patterns defeated her. She confessed her failure to me and to her group. She was clearly discouraged and angry with herself for her lack of progress.

I reminded Carrie that it would take time to turn her whole life around and establish new patterns. So she persevered. The next week she had two successful days in which she spent quality time with God, planned out her day, finished most of her work, and avoided temptation. The next week she had five good days—and the week after that, seven. Through it all, I saw Carrie's confidence begin to grow, and she began to *glow* in her appearance and her accomplishments.

Together we developed techniques to help Carrie avoid overindulging on food and TV. She began making firm "no" choices at the grocery store so she didn't need to face the choice at her refrigerator door. She pulled the exercise bicycle out of the garage, dusted it off, and started daily aerobic exercise. Following her doctor's advice, Carrie began pedaling ten minutes each day and gradually worked up to 25 minutes of daily exercise. She began to shed pounds, and every little change in her appearance made a *big* change in the way she saw herself.

During her "withdrawal" phase, Carrie kept the TV unplugged, replacing soap operas with Christian radio programs and music. She also scheduled a slot of time for herself—that last peaceful half-hour before her two boys came bounding in from school. During this special "quality time" with herself, she ignored the phone and doorbell, devoting herself to good books and music. "I hadn't done much reading since college," she said, "so it was rewarding to begin to *learn* again. I read books on parenting by Ross Campbell and James Dobson. And a book by Sybil Stanton, *The 25 Hour Woman*, taught me how to prioritize, make decisions, and develop a life purpose for myself."

As we continued to meet together, Carrie realized that her self-confidence was founded on being an accepted, beloved child of God, even though she felt her late father had rejected her. Moreover, she recognized that she was really more successful and capable than her low self-image could admit—as a mother, as a wife, as a Sunday school teacher, and as a friend to others.

Through the affirmation of Christian friends, Carrie learned how much she was loved and valued for the unique and special woman of God she was. She began to stretch herself in new directions—working in her church to develop new ministries for women, and working with community organizations such as Big Brothers and Big Sisters.

Today Carrie is a woman with a purpose. She is gradually gaining a healthy self-image and growing in her understanding of the special gifts and abilities God has given her. From a place of malaise and quiet desperation, Carrie has achieved a place of meaning and direction. God has given her a new beginning, and she has seized that new beginning as an opportunity to launch out into the adventure of life.

I've seen it happen again and again. People come to a point in life where they feel abandoned by God, set aside, and worthless, like a cracked teacup relegated to a dusty shelf. But God is not through with you and me. Whether we feel his presence or not, he is alongside us, weaving all the circumstances of our lives together into his plan. No matter how far down we go, he is never through with us. He lifts us up and invites us to begin again.

God is not through with the unemployed father who has spent months looking for a job, whose unemployment insurance is running out, and who faces the prospect of providing for his family with hands that are completely empty.

God is not through with the unmarried young woman, a church youth worker, who is pregnant.

God is not through with the "work-oholic" businessman who has lost the love and respect of his children through years of neglecting them.

God is not through with the wife who has fallen into adultery and betrayed the trust of her husband and little children.

God is not through with the businessman whose reputation and testimony for Christ have been badly tarnished by a vicious rumor.

God is not through with the middle-aged widow who faces the future alone, suddenly aware that her life—once defined by her relationship to her husband—has no definition or direction at all since his death.

And God is not through with *you*. He offers you an invitation. Even though it may look like the end for you, our God is the God of the resurrection, the God of a new beginning—*and he invites you to begin again.*

3

The Glue

Today he's a mended man. But just a few years ago, my friend Elliot thought his life was over.

Elliot was arrested on a serious morals charge involving an underage girl. As a result, he lost his executive position with a major defense contractor in California's "Silicon Valley." Former friends and associates shunned him. He narrowly avoided a jail term. His self-image was shattered, replaced by unrelenting shame and hopelessness.

"I have a gun at home that I bought for protection," Elliot told me. "I've taken it out and looked it over, thinking how nice it would be to feel nothing at all instead of feeling so shameful and guilty. The only thing that kept me from pulling the trigger was thinking about my wife and my little boys. How could I hurt them even more than I already have?"

I've rarely seen as much anguish and remorse in one human being as I saw in my friend Elliot. "I hate myself for what I did," he confessed to me. "To me, it's the worst sin in the world. You say God can forgive me, Ron, but I don't know. I just know I'll never forgive myself. I'm going to pay for this mistake for the rest of my life. And I think that's the way it should be."

After being fired, Elliot applied for dozens of jobs in the same field. Routine background checks invariably turned up his arrest record. Sometimes the rejections were accompanied by a tersely worded reference to "certain events" in his past. Sometimes they simply stated that the position had been filled. On one occasion his application was returned with an acidly worded note berating him for his "obvious character deficiencies" and the "conspicuously sordid" nature of his past. If ever a man needed a new beginning in life, if ever a man needed to grasp the deepest meaning of the word *grace*, it was my friend Elliot.

The more I talk to people, both inside and outside the Church, the more I realize how little people understand what grace really means. Grace: when we don't deserve love, we are unconditionally loved. Grace: when we sin so spectacularly that we think ourselves to be unforgivable, we are forgiven. Grace: when we deserve a lifetime of misery and an eternity of separation from God, we are given a new chance in life and an eternity in the loving presence of God.

The most amazing gift of grace we have received from God is the gift of his Son, Jesus Christ. Grace penetrated this sick and sorrowing world in a new and profound way on that first Christmas. We tend to think of Christmas as that annual ritual remembering the baby Jesus rocking in his cradle while shepherds and wise men smiled their best Hallmark smiles. To us Christmas means singing all the old familiar carols and buying out Macy's and Toys "R" Us to the bare walls.

But the gift of God's grace is forever, not just for the 25th day of each December. Seen from God's perspective, every day of the year is Christmas. By the infinite grace of God, there's a surprise under the tree every morning. We just have to take it, open it, and look inside.

The good news of the Christian gospel is that Jesus is the tangible expression of God's grace to us. Jesus was not just a baby in a manger, a respected moral teacher, or the founder of one of the great religions of the world. The little baby in the manger of straw was ultimately God made flesh, the expression of God's grace. He is the one who could very well say, "I died upon that cross of wood, but I made the hill on which it stood."

Over and over in the Gospels we see that the ministry of Jesus was a ministry of grace. He was the gift of a new beginning to all mankind. Jesus took ruined lives and gave them value, meaning, and dignity again. By grace he touched the life of a sin-ridden woman by a well in Samaria, and that woman was never the same again. By grace he spared an adulterous woman from being stoned by an angry mob. He forgave her sin and told her to sin no more. By grace he forgave those who tortured him to death upon a cross. By grace he told a repentant, crucified thief, "Today you will be with me in paradise." By grace he healed lepers, a nobleman's son, the demon-afflicted, the lame, the palsied, the blind. Jesus' ministry was grace upon grace upon grace. He came into the world, declared the apostle John, "full of grace and truth."

If you're lacking joy right now, if you're staggering under the weight of guilt and regret, then you need the touch of God's grace. But you're not alone. We are all needy, all hurting, and all in need of a new beginning.

Some years ago I was leading a class of 30 adults. Most of the class members had been Christians for a number of years and were growing in their faith. One Sunday I posed a question to the group: "Imagine that Jesus was outside our door, ready to step inside this room and meet you face-to-face. How would you feel about being in the physical presence of Jesus Christ?" Twenty-nine of my class members responded that their primary feeling would be one of fear and inadequacy. Some said they would even feel ashamed.

But one class member, a young man named Larry, said he would feel joy, excitement, and anticipation in Christ's presence. Larry told us he would run to Jesus and embrace him.

He imagined that the Lord would say to him, "Larry, I love you. You've fumbled the ball a few times. You've made your mistakes. You've fallen short. But I love you." In a room full of dedicated Christians, only one young man demonstrated a clear understanding of God's grace.

We all need a deeper understanding of the grace of God. Someone once wrote, "Man is born broken. He lives by mending, and the grace of God is the glue." It's true. The grace of God is the glue that makes broken people whole—and who among us is not broken in some area of his or her life, spirit, or personality?

My friend Elliot has been learning more and more about the grace of God. He's learning to know and trust the God of a new beginning. Elliot knows that it was the grace of God that allowed him to be arrested, lose his career, and tumble into the depths of helplessness and depression. God didn't tempt Elliot to sin. But God was able to turn the consequences of his sin into something beautiful: *a transformed life*.

Before his fall, Elliot was proud and self-assured. His work was his world. Though he had been raised in a religious family, God played a very small role in his life. After his fall, Elliot suddenly had nothing to cling to, no one to turn to, and no hope in the world except God alone. His shattering experience caused him to see his need of God and feel his total helplessness apart from God. It was grace that saved my friend from self-reliant, self-destructive pride.

Elliot never regained his previous career, but he found a good job in another field. He earns less money and enjoys less prestige—but is able to spend more time with his family. His values are different now. Being with his wife and children is far more important to him than pursuing career ambitions.

Elliot's relationship with God is now foremost. A few years ago he couldn't have named the four Gospels. Today he studies the Bible regularly and avidly.

In the course of Elliot's healing process, I encouraged him to talk with a friend of mine, a Christian counselor. At first

Elliot resisted the suggestion, feeling that seeking counseling was a sign of weakness. A few vestiges of his old pride, it seemed, still clung to him. But over a few weeks he came to understand that his real weakness was his refusal to reach out for competent help. So Elliot received counseling. And with the help of his counselor, and the support of his wife and a few Christian friends, Elliot began to mend—day by day, a little bit at a time—and the grace of God was the glue.

Today my friend Elliot is actively involved in the ministry of a church. He has regained his self-respect. He is a spiritual leader and positive role-model in his family. He has experienced the grace and forgiveness of God in a powerful way. Elliot is living proof of the transforming equation: *Failure + the grace of God = a new beginning*. The word *grace* is being defined in his life daily.

For Elliot, each morning is the beginning of a new adventure in his journey of faith. And there's an adventure ahead of you as well. The road awaits you. I wish you courage, faith, and boldness on your journey.

4

When Life Is Not Fair

Pastor Hayes, a man in his middle forties, was well-loved by his congregation, and faithful to God and to his family. He enjoyed a successful ministry in an exuberantly vital, growing church. Just when everything seemed to be going well, a cloud came over this man and his ministry.

Rumors circulated through the church that Pastor Hayes was guilty of moral misconduct. He had been seen at the home of Miss Morrow, a school teacher, just a few weeks before she resigned for "personal reasons" and moved to another city. Apparently someone in the church put two and two together—and came up with five.

Pastor Hayes was innocent, but the stain of the alleged scandal could not be erased. The rumors followed Pastor Hayes for years, seriously hampering his effectiveness as a pastor. It was difficult for him to endure the rejection, mistreatment, and misunderstanding caused by the false rumors. But it was even more difficult for him to witness the toll of these events on his wife and on his teenaged son.

It was ten years later—after his son graduated from college—that Pastor Hayes learned how the hurtful rumors began. One night a man the pastor had not seen for years appeared at his door. "Brother McLean!" said Pastor Hayes in surprise. "I haven't seen you in..."

"Eight years," McLean supplied. "It's been eight years since I left the church." McLean had been an elder in the church, but left a few months after his term expired. Pastor Hayes studied McLean's features. He looked older, and something was clearly troubling him. "Please come in," the pastor invited warmly.

"No," McLean answered quickly, "I only have a few minutes to talk. I just had to tell you—I was the one responsible."

"What? I don't...."

"The story about you and Miss Morrow," McLean interrupted. "I was the one who started it all."

"You!" Pastor Hayes' hands and voice trembled as old emotions flooded back. "But why? You knew I was innocent, didn't you? Miss Morrow left town to care for her dying father. She called me to her house the day she learned of her father's cancer. I went there to pray with her. How could you twist that into...."

"I know! I know!" Tears began to fill the other man's eyes. "*I* was twisted, Pastor! Twisted with jealousy! You see, before you came, I was a *leader* in this church. The previous pastor asked my advice on everything. People looked up to me. The programs I was involved in were flourishing.

"But when you came, a lot of new people came into the church. There were so many new programs and people didn't listen to my ideas anymore. The church got so big—and it took a different direction. I felt left behind. I was so angry and bitter against you. Pastor Hayes, I don't expect you to forgive me, but I just had to tell you."

The pastor stepped toward the man who had deeply hurt him for ten years. He wrapped his arms around Mr. McLean and embraced him. There in the yellow glow of the porch light, McLean sobbed away years of pent-up sorrow and guilt in the arms of the man he had wronged. And Pastor Hayes

held him with the strong arms of forgiveness and unconditional love, saying repeatedly, "I forgive you, my brother. I
forgive you."

Life is not fair. Mistreatment, misunderstanding, and
rejection stalk us throughout our lives. You may presently be
enduring the pain of your reputation being destroyed. Perhaps the minds of people in your church or community—even
family members and friends—have been poisoned against
you. You may be experiencing mistreatment and rejection on
a continual basis—on the job, in your church, or from a
family member. No matter what you say or do, or how pure
your motives are, there will be times when you will be treated
unfairly.

In times of unfair treatment, we desperately need to gain
God's perspective on life. And the source of his perspective is
the Bible. A primary lesson we learn about life from the Bible
is that trials of mistreatment are not rare occurrences. Injustice is the order of the day—especially for those who are
seeking to follow Christ. "Blessed are you," Jesus said in
Matthew 5:11, "when people insult you, persecute you and
falsely say all kinds of evil against you because of me." And
Peter, in 1 Peter 4:12, wrote, "Dear friends, do not be surprised at the painful trial you are suffering, as though
something strange were happening to you." In order to survive in such a harsh world, we need to understand the grace
of the God of a new beginning.

It's normal to feel inner pain when we are rejected and
mistreated. It's normal to wonder why we must suffer so
unfairly. Why couldn't God take us *around* our trials instead
of *through* them? Well, God *could* lead us around our trials.
But if he did so, how could we grow from the experience? How
could we become more like Christ?

Paul gave us a principle for responding to suffering in
Philippians 3:10: "I want to know Christ and the power of his
resurrection and the fellowship of sharing in his sufferings,
becoming like him in his death." And 1 Peter 4:13 encourages

us to "rejoice that you participate in the sufferings of Christ, so that you may be overjoyed when his glory is revealed." As we learn to rely upon God through our trials of unfair treatment, we become more like Christ. And it was Jesus Christ, the completely innocent and righteous man, who endured for our sakes a level of rejection and mistreatment far beyond human comprehension.

Someone once said that God is not the author of sin, but he is never surprised by it. The God of a New Beginning is able to take our deepest hurts and weave them into a pattern of beauty and meaning for our lives. As we grow in our experience of the new-beginning grace of God, we gain more and more of God's perspective on the trials we face.

Life is like a river which flows to the sea. God sees the river from above, watching its windings and turnings, its foaming rapids and perilous falls, its placid pools and backwaters. We sail the river of life like boats caught in the current. We can never see farther than the next bend. But God sees the river of life all the way from the headwaters to the place where it flows into the vast ocean of his love. Because he has the entire map of our journey before him, we can trust him to steer us safely through the narrows and to keep us afloat through the rapids.

Kierkegaard once said, "Life can only be understood backwards; but it must be lived forwards." You are living life in the forward direction, with limited perspective and limited understanding. Someday you will be able to look backward, and the circumstances of your life that seem so painful and baffling now will blend into a beautiful and meaningful pattern. The purpose of your trial of rejection, so dark and inscrutable today, will one day be made clear.

Our lives seem to oscillate between peace and turbulence, pleasure and pain. Whether you are up or down right now, the key to stability in life is *reliance upon God.* If you don't rely on him in times of elation, when everything is going well, you may become proud and self-satisfied, with no need for

God. And if you do not rely on him in times of rejection and trial, then you will probably become bitter, depressed, and fearful of the future.

God is building a stable, proven character in our lives that is strong in both good times and bad. You will never know that kind of stability if you rely on people rather than God for the shaping of your attitude. People may elate you—or they may depress you. They may love you—or they may reject you. If your outlook is dependent on how people treat you rather than on God's unchanging, unconditional love, your life will be an emotional roller coaster ride—a wild journey in which the ups may not begin to compensate for the downs.

Lloyd Ogilvie said, "One rejection can tip the scales weighted with hundreds of affirmations." It's true. The rebuff of *one* person can easily cancel out *all* the positive strokes we receive in our lives. That's why I keep a certain manila folder in my file cabinet. That folder is filed under "E" for "Encouragement." It contains more than a hundred letters I have accumulated over the years. On those blue Mondays, when I feel pressured or accused by people, or when my self-image is sagging, I reach for my encouragement file and pull out a letter. Those letters comfort me, affirm me, and restore my perspective. Positive words from others enable me endure rejection and persevere.

The apostle Paul knew what it was like to face rejection. He was beaten, imprisoned, jeered, and even stoned—literally buried under a crushing pile of rocks and left for dead. He experienced a level of rejection few other Christians have faced. Paul's attitude did not depend on how people treated him, but on how God unconditionally accepted him. Writing about the rejection and persecution he experienced on his missionary travels, Paul stated in 2 Corinthians 1:8-9, "We were under great pressure, far beyond our ability to endure, so that we despaired even of life. Indeed, in our hearts we felt the sentence of death. But this happened that we might not rely on ourselves but on God."

Life's highs and lows, mountains and valleys, affirmations and rejections just keep coming. We will only find stability and peace in our lives as we learn to rely completely and solely on the Lord.

An essential quality for withstanding unfair treatment is a healthy sense of self-worth which is rooted—and this is the key—in a close relationship to God. A sense of self-worth which is rooted in how others rate us, or in our own righteousness and achievement, is doomed to falter when we are mistreated or when we fail. But when we base our sense of self-worth on God's unconditional acceptance, then we can truly accept ourselves. And the more accepting we are of ourselves, the less vulnerable we become to the rejection of others.

Kathy was a high school student I met at a church I served in the Midwest. Shortly after she moved to our community and started attending our church, rumors began to spread about her. Kathy reportedly had very loose morals. The rumor also hinted that she had an abortion in the city she moved from.

But Kathy had been unfairly treated. The rumors were untrue. We learned later that the source of the rumors, a woman in our church, had confused Kathy with another girl. But just as there's no way to unscramble an egg, there was no way to undo the damage to Kathy's reputation. It was something she had to learn to live with.

How do you learn to endure the rejection and unfair treatment of others? The first key is to avoid focusing on the situation. If the injustice you are experiencing absorbs your thoughts and your emotions, you will become filled with bitter, long-term anger that will gnaw at your vitals. If you can't let go of that anger, it will inevitably consume you.

Life is a vast adventure filled with great dreams, great experiences, and great things to enjoy. Your life must be larger than the injustices you face. If you allow those injustices to so distort your outlook that you miss the joy of knowing God, of having fellowship with family and friends, and of enjoying the good things that God has graciously given us in this life, then you have given your persecutors enormous power over you. You have allowed them to overshadow your life, to control your attitude, and to steal your joy. But if you can keep your gaze on the important things in life—the relationships, loves, and pleasures that give you joy—then the outlines of your unjust ordeal will shrink to their true proportions.

The second key to enduring unfair treatment is to avoid focusing on yourself. If self is your focus in a time of trial, you will become filled with self-pity. The Christian life is to be lived in an attitude of thanks and praise to God your loving Father. Self-absorption and self-pity are attitude traits that are completely inconsistent with the grace, forgiveness, and love you have received so abundantly from God. When you are ill-treated by others, learn to pray, "God, please help me see this person as a tool in your hands, not as an enemy. Help me see this person as part of your process of shaping my character. Thank you that I am your handiwork and that you are using *even this* in my life to make me more mature and more Christlike."

Third, avoid blaming others. If blame is your focus in a time of trial, you'll never be able to see past your grudges to discover the grace of God. The God of a new beginning calls us to express toward others the same quality of grace we have received from him. He calls us to forgiveness, not bitterness. As Paul wrote in Romans 12:17-21,

> Do not repay anyone evil for evil.... If it is possible, as far as it depends on you, live at peace with everyone. Do not take revenge, my friends, but leave room for God's wrath, for it is written: "It is mine to avenge; I will repay," says the Lord. On the contrary: "If your enemy is hungry, feed him; if he is thirsty, give him something to drink. In doing this, you will heap burning coals on his head." Do

not be overcome by evil, but overcome evil with good.

In this way, we show others the same new-beginning grace God has shown us.

Finally, stop defending yourself. This spiritual key goes against our instinct for self-preservation. When we are attacked, we naturally want to put up a fight or erect a defense. Yet often when we feel a desperate need to clear our names, a defense is impossible. At such times we need to learn to let God be our defender.

One of my favorite authors, A.W. Tozer, once wrote a booklet called *Seven Secrets to Spiritual Power*. One of Tozer's seven secrets was, "Never defend yourself." We must defend the Gospel, we must defend those who have no defense, but we must not be anxious to defend ourselves. If there is misunderstanding, then we should seek to bring clarity and understanding to the situation. But we don't need to justify ourselves anymore. We have already been justified by grace through faith in Jesus Christ. He is our defender, and we no longer need to feel defensive for ourselves.

If we keep our minds and hearts open and teachable, God will be able to use all the experiences in our lives—including the pain of rejection and unfair treatment—to shape us into the kind of people he desires us to be. When we are rejected, we are to be people of forgiveness and grace—people who shoulder the responsibilities for our own faults while overlooking the faults of others.

God knows what he is doing, even when we are unjustly treated. Though life must be lived forward, one day we will look backward—and we will understand.

5

A Matter of Time

As I write these words, it has been about two years since I lost my only brother to cancer. Paul Davis was my best friend. His death at age 41 left an aching void in my heart and my life. I don't believe the old cliché, "Time heals all wounds." Time has eased *some* of the sting and intensity of my grief. But I still feel the pain of this loss.

About three weeks after my brother's memorial service, a man in my church made an appointment to see me. He was a friend and a well-meaning fellow Christian. I had no idea what he wanted to talk about, but as we sat down in my counseling room he got right to the point.

"You know, Ron," he began, "you're not only a Christian, you're also the pastor of this church. And as the pastor, you are to be a model of the joy and victory we have because of the resurrection of Christ. Your brother was a believer, so you know he's in heaven and that you'll be reunited with him in eternity. So I think it's time you put your grief behind you." This, only three weeks after my brother's death.

I know this man came to me because he sincerely loved me and cared about my spiritual condition. But he had never lost a close family member and had no real conception of what I was going through. Though he honestly tried to help me, his words brought more hurt than healing.

Healing is a matter of time. The deeper the wound, the greater the amount of time we need to recover. If you have been through a serious hurt like a divorce, a scandal, a severe legal problem, or the loss of a career, you will need time—a lot of time—to heal.

Like so many in contemporary society, you may have bought into the idea that there is a quick fix to every problem. Got a headache? Get fast relief with this or that brand of aspirin. Hungry? Fast food is the answer. Ten items or less, use the express line—no waiting. You can drink instant coffee, prepare an instant dinner in your microwave, and withdraw instant money from the automatic teller. You can turn on your TV and find instant inspiration from today's electronic church. We live in an age of instant gratification. So when life begins to hurt a little, we expect instant relief. We want the pain to stop *now*. But the cold, hard facts of life do not always accommodate our expectations.

If someone close to us is going through an extended period of pain and recovery, we sometimes wonder, "Why doesn't he just snap out of it? How long can one person stay depressed?" Or, "She's been divorced for a year now. You'd think she could stop mooning around and get on with her life!"

"Snap out of it! Grow up! Get on with it!" Unfeeling words like these have been directed to me and to many other hurting people. Perhaps someone has spoken them to you. The fact is, every individual is different. The time frame for healing is a little different for each of us. We commit an injustice when we box another person into our time frame.

You may find that people will support you, visit you, call you, and care for you during the first few weeks of a painful time in your life. But I think you will also find that only a few people will continue to care for you over the long haul of your recovery. It seems to me that while a person's experience of grief and pain may be long-term, the caring response of many Christians is usually short-term. So the hurting individual is often left to deal with his problems alone.

Our struggle to find a new beginning in life is all too often a lonely struggle. The people around us don't seem to understand us or our problems. Some merely keep their distance from us; others turn their backs on us. We feel abandoned and invisible in our churches, and even in our own families. It's like being a castaway on a desolate island, left utterly alone with our pain—and with time, interminable hours and days of time.

A few years ago, a classified advertisement in a Midwest newspaper offered: "I will listen to you talk for 30 minutes, without comment, for $10." This was a legitimate offer made by a man who understood the powerful needs within the lonely heart. The ad was enormously successful. The man received a minimum of 20 calls a day. The pain of loneliness is so profound that it drives some people to pay money to an anonymous stranger for a few minutes of non-judgmental listening.

Loneliness takes its toll on us physically as well as emotionally. Though I am normally very conscientious about my daily exercise and diet, the grief and loneliness I felt after my brother's death led me to neglect my physical needs. I became careless about eating and I stopped running in the mornings. I gained 15 pounds. A chronic digestive disorder, which I can usually control with diet and relaxation, flared up seriously during this time. It's a common pattern: people going through a period of loneliness often neglect themselves physically.

When God finished creating the world, he looked at everything he made and declared that it was good. Only once in the creation narrative does God mention anything that is *not* good. Genesis 2:18 records his words: "It is not good for the man to be alone." God knew how painful loneliness would be for his human creation.

"Loneliness," observes Neil Straight, "is spending your days alone with your thoughts, your discouragements. It is having no one with whom to share your life." Loneliness is not cured by surrounding yourself with a great number of people. Rather, loneliness is cured by investing yourself and your time in a few intimate friends.

One of my joys as a pastor is greeting people at the door after a worship service. But in the days immediately following Paul's death, the greeting time was an ordeal for me. There I was with a multitude of people, most of whom genuinely cared for me and understood my hurt. They struggled to find the right words to express their love and sympathy to me. There were moments of warmth and moments of awkwardness. But for me it was mostly a time of loneliness. As much as I appreciated the expressions of sympathy from the hundreds of people who filed by each Sunday, I didn't want to be with the multitude.

The greatest help I received in my time of loneliness was from a handful of intimate friends with whom I could be totally authentic and transparent about my feelings. I'm grateful for the fellowship of a few Christians who were "unshockable," who listened to my doubts, who empathized with me, and who were always available. When you have two or three friends like that, you are blessed.

Loneliness can be a prison. The apostle Paul understood the prison of loneliness, for he experienced the depths of loneliness within a literal prison. Though accustomed to traveling extensively throughout the known world in his ministry, toward the end of his life Paul found himself confined in a Roman dungeon. The apostle was physically locked away from the people he loved—and who loved him.

What was Paul's response to the lonely isolation of prison? Did he give up in despair? Did he quit his ministry? Did he pity himself and bemoan his fate? No! Paul transformed his imprisonment and loneliness into ministry to others. He purposefully launched into a number of activities which obliterated his prison walls and dispelled his loneliness. Paul's response to his loneliness is a good example for those of us who feel locked away from others. First, Paul wrote letters. He reached out over the miles to maintain human contact with his friends. Writing letters is a good antidote for our loneliness too. Paul didn't have a telephone, but if he had, he probably would have used it to keep in touch with his friends. A phone can be a communication lifeline during a time of loneliness.

Second, Paul served others. From his cramped prison cell, he wrote four particular letters of potent encouragement— Ephesians, Philippians, Colossians, and Philemon—which have blessed literally millions of readers down through the centuries. As historian James Stalker observed, "Paul converted his one room in Rome into a far-reaching mission for Christ. On the few feet of space that was allowed him, he erected a fulcrum from which he would now move the world." Paul resisted the temptation to retreat further into his isolation, choosing instead to reach out and encourage others. This is a choice that you and I can make as well.

Third, Paul spent time with good books. In 2 Timothy 4:13, Paul instructed his fellow missionary: "When you come, bring . . . my scrolls, especially the parchments." Paul recognized that his lonely prison time was an opportunity to enrich himself mentally and spiritually. Paul knew the companionship of good books which, like good friends, provide the pleasure of enriching thoughts, feelings, and experiences. Though advancing in years, Paul would not put his mind in retirement.

I can identify with Paul in his love for books. In my times of loneliness since my brother's death, good books—especially the Book of books, the Bible—have been a source of companionship, consolation, and strength for me. I have been enriched by such authors as A.W. Tozer, Charles Colson, Oswald Chambers, C.S. Lewis, Henri Nouwen, and Chuck Swindoll. In books by these and other great writers, I find insights for my trial and an intimate connection to great minds and kindred hearts. This connection is like a bridge which transcends my feelings of isolation.

How are you handling your trial of loneliness? If you've been through an experience of great hurt, allow yourself some time to heal. Then, as you gain God's perspective on your trial, take steps to transcend it, transform it, and stretch yourself beyond it. Reach out to a few trusted friends and pull them close. Pray with them. Share your hurts, joys, and needs with them. You can either discover creative ways for transcending your loneliness, or you can surrender to self-pity and bitterness. The choice is yours.

My prayer is that you invest your healing time wisely, and that you will live all your life as a hymn of praise and thanks to the God of a new beginning.

6

Dead End or New Beginning?

At the height of World War II, the British army was tenaciously entrenched in North Africa to defend the strategic Suez Canal from capture by the Germans. But in early 1942, General Erwin Rommel, Hitler's notorious "Desert Fox," began a drive across the sands of Libya, his eye fixed on Egypt and the Suez. The British fought valiantly, but to no avail. First Banghazi fell to the advancing Germans, then Tobruk. Finally, Rommel's forces rolled victoriously into Egypt.

The British troops were demoralized and their armored tank force decimated. Retreating hundreds of miles before Rommel's furious assault, the British stood with their backs to the Suez, facing a foe of seemingly supernatural cunning and ferocity.

In August 1942, General Bernard L. Montgomery took field command of the beleaguered British 8th Army in Egypt. Montgomery was a jaunty, infectiously optimistic man and a brilliant field tactician. But he seemed extraordinarily subdued the day he and a subordinate climbed a dune to scout Rommel's encampment at el-Alamein.

"Ah, it's a sad thing," Montgomery sighed, "that a professional soldier should reach the peak of generalship, then suffer the defeat which dashes his career."

The subordinate, alarmed to see the normally exuberant commander in such a downcast mood, said, "Don't be depressed, sir. We may still win through."

The general flashed a sudden grin. "Of course we shall win through, old boy! I wasn't feeling sorry for myself. I was talking about Rommel!"

History records that Montgomery rallied his troops, routed Rommel's forces, and drove the Germans eastward clear across North Africa. The Desert Fox never won another battle on the African desert.

The British snatched a stunning victory from a disastrous defeat partly because of the courageous, positive attitude of General Montgomery. The same can be true for you and me. The key to victory when we feel like our backs are against the wall is our *attitude*.

What is your attitude toward life? Do you see yourself as a victim? Do you feel like people and circumstances are holding you down, preventing you from achieving growth and change? Do you blame others for your failure? Do you look at the road ahead and think, *I just can't go on anymore*? If so, one obstacle that may be hindering your discovery of God's new beginning is your attitude toward life.

Think for a moment of a major barrier which sits like a roadblock across the path of your life: a lost job, a lost marriage, a ruined reputation, a broken relationship. Imagine that there is a sign tacked to that barrier. What does it say? "Stop"? "Wrong Way"? "Dead End"?

It's time to replace that sign. Envision, instead, a sign on your barrier that says "Detour." Our disappointments and discouragements must be viewed as *detours* instead of dead ends. Dead ends stop us in our tracks. But detours redirect us toward unexpected and rewarding destinations. A detour in life can be a fascinating journey, full of new discoveries and challenging insights, if we will only open our eyes to see the possibilities God is presenting to us.

It has been said that when God shuts a door, he opens a window. So when the door slams shut on your plans and expectations, it's time to look for that open window of opportunity. It's a window that will never be found in the gloom of a negative attitude. It's a window that can only be seen with eyes of faith—faith in God's goodness, faith in his plan for our lives, and faith in his power to transform our lives. To have an attitude of faith means to trust the God of a new beginning to bring about a fresh start in your life.

When you decide to become serious about finding God's new-beginning grace for your life, you will begin to demonstrate several specific attitudes. First, you will have a *prayerful attitude*. In Matthew 7:7-8, Jesus tells us that in order to receive, we must ask; to find, we must seek; to enter the door, we must knock. In short, we must be people of prayer. We must participate in regular dialogue with the God of a new beginning, seeking from him the grace we need for each day.

Jesus goes on to tell us, in Matthew 7:9-11, that our loving Father gives nothing but good gifts. "Which of you," he asks, "if his son asks for bread, will give him a stone? Or if he asks for a fish, will give him a snake? If you, then, though you are evil, know how to give good gifts to your children, how much more will your Father in heaven give good gifts to those who ask him!" By faith we recognize that God always answers our prayers, giving us his very best gifts. At the same time, we recognize that God is sovereign; he is in control. So we listen carefully and sensitively for the precise answer he chooses to give us—even if he answers our prayers in ways we are not expecting. Our attitude should be one of flexibility, openness, and readiness to receive God's grace in whatever shape and size package he sends it in.

A six-year-old boy lost his favorite toy car and looked all over the house for it without success. Finally he asked his mother if it would be all right to ask God to help him find his car.

"Of course, Honey," she replied. "You can talk to God about anything." So the boy scampered off to his bedroom to talk to God.

Later the mother saw her son playing in the backyard with a soccer ball. The toy car was nowhere in sight. Wondering about her son's prayer, she called out, "Honey, did God help you find your car?"

The boy ran up to her with the soccer ball in his hands. "No," he said with a broad grin, "but he made me want to play with this soccer ball instead!"

When we cultivate the pliable faith-attitude demonstrated by this little boy, we will see God's responses to our prayers in a new way. Whether he gives us what we want or not, God always gives us what we need—his very best gifts, his grace, and his plan for a new beginning in life. Even when there are circumstances and trials in our lives that do not change, we still can choose to allow those circumstances and trials to *change us*, to change our desires into conformity with his will and to mold us into the kind of people he wants us to become.

Second, when you become serious about finding God's new-beginning grace for your life, you will demonstrate an *attitude of honesty*. You will courageously face the truth about yourself. You won't hide from the fact that sin is sin. You won't say that you got into a "difficult situation." You won't euphemize sin as an "error in judgment." You won't blame others. You will honestly confess to God and to yourself that there is sin, there is failure, and there are character defects in your life. Until you accurately recognize, admit, and own your problem, you are powerless to solve it.

Greg and Kurt were brothers, sons of an alcoholic father. Their father frequently abused the boys and their mother physically and verbally. He squandered much of the family's meager income on his addiction to drink. When the boys were teenagers, their father left the family and was never heard from again.

Greg somehow managed to transcend his painful childhood and he grew up to be a loving Christian husband and father. He never touched alcohol. And he enjoyed the respect and admiration of his community. Kurt, however, became a carbon copy of his father: abusive, violent, and addicted to alcohol. Like his father, Kurt abandoned his wife and children, and moved to a shelter for homeless men.

A social worker interviewed Kurt and learned, as she expected, that Kurt's tragic life-style was a product of his equally tragic past. When she asked him why he thought his life had turned out so miserably, Kurt replied, "How else would you expect me to turn out, with a father like mine?"

The social worker then interviewed Greg. When she asked Greg why he thought his life had turned out so happily despite his family background, he replied: "How else would you expect me to turn out, with a father like mine?"

There was one essential difference between these two brothers: a difference in attitude, a difference in honesty, a difference in willingness to accept responsibility and face the truth about oneself.

"If we claim to be without sin," reads 1 John 1:8, "we deceive ourselves and the truth is not in us." We have an enormous capacity for self-deception and for denying the sin within us. And it is this inability to face the truth about ourselves that hinders us from appropriating God's new-beginning grace for our lives. As Keith Miller observes in *Sin: Overcoming the Ultimate Deadly Addiction,*

> We must discover a way to focus a clear light into the dark and shadowy regions of our lives where we have buried specific sins and character defects and hidden them even from ourselves. These buried things from our past make us very touchy. They operate like mines in an uncharted mine field protecting the citadel of our Sin. These buried sin-mines explode in fear and anger when someone innocently steps on one of them. We need to see and

own these hidden sins and character defects so that we can bring them out and surrender them to God in confession. Then, as he takes them and forgives us, the feeling of "danger" evaporates for us and the people around us....

We begin by cleaning out the debris of the past by making a thorough examination of our own lives and bringing what we find out into the light (see 1 John 1:5-9). We are to face our character defects and moral transgressions with all the thoroughness we can put together and with rigorous honesty. But we are also to include in our inventory the positive character traits and abilities that God has given us. These are the assets through which he will work to fight the [disease of our sin].[1]

Third, when you become serious about finding God's new-beginning grace for your life, you will demonstrate an *attentive attitude*. Many of us go through life without really reflecting on where we are going and where we have been. We make decisions without planning or thinking through to the consequences. We live through our days making scores of decisions, yet we seem to be too busy to attentively think about our decisions. Yet neglecting to reflect, consider, and plan can lead us right back into the patterns of past failures.

A surgeon once said that if he had only four minutes to perform a life-saving operation, he would spend the first minute examining the patient and planning the procedure. Certainly our pressures are not so great that we should be any less attentive to the choices we face in our own lives.

Fourth, when you become serious about finding God's new-beginning grace for your life, you will demonstrate a *responsible attitude*. You will realize that you alone are responsible for your own choices, your own experiences, and your own results. God has given you a new beginning in life; it is up to you to take that opportunity and make the most of it. When you have a responsible attitude, you make the choice *not* to be a victim of circumstances, *not* to be a victim of other people, and *not* to be a victim of your failed past. Instead of a victim, you choose to be a *victor*. No one else can be responsible for your life; your life is your responsibility.

℣ John Powell, one of my favorite Christian writers, said that he keeps a card taped to his mirror. It's positioned so that he cannot avoid seeing it every morning. Its message: "You are now looking at the face of the person who is responsible for your happiness today." Not others, not circumstances, not the past—you alone are responsible for your choices, your responses, your sins, and ultimately your happiness. God gives you the opportunity for a new beginning with each new day. But it is your responsibility to seize the opportunity and live your life victoriously.

Fifth, when you become serious about finding God's new-beginning grace for your life, you will demonstrate a *determined attitude*. You will make agreements with yourself and you will keep those agreements. You will agree with yourself to avoid those temptations that led you into failure before. You will agree with yourself to maintain certain disciplines that will enable you to grow—spiritual disciplines of prayer and Bible study; physical disciplines of diet and exercise; mental and emotional disciplines of reading good books, nurturing relationships, and seeking professional counseling.

Make sure that the agreements you make with yourself are reasonable and do-able. Don't set yourself up for failure with unreasonable expectations. When you fail, confess it to God, ask for his help to keep going, and get back in there and persevere with that agreement. One of the most serious consequences of breaking agreements with ourselves is that we then fall into the trap of blaming and judging ourselves. We think, *I can't do it*. We see ourselves as failures, and our self-image begins to break down.

You *can* keep your agreements with yourself. You *can* grow. You *can* recover from the failures of the past. You *can* have the attitude of the apostle Paul, who said in Philippians 4:13 (NASB), "I can do all things through him who strengthens me."

John Powell tells of a time he was driving on a busy Chicago freeway and his car ran out of gas. He was already late for a meeting, and now he obviously wasn't going to arrive at all. Frustrated and angry, Powell decided to sit in the car and wait until someone came along and helped him. Someone finally stopped and helped him get some gasoline, and several hours later he arrived home. He was tired, dirty, and grumpy. He had missed his meeting and his day was pretty well ruined.

A few days later, Powell was in another meeting when a co-worker of his, Mrs. Brady, walked in about 30 minutes late. "I'm sorry I'm late," she said. "I had a little car trouble." After the meeting, Powell asked Mrs. Brady about her car trouble.

"Well, it's kind of embarrassing," she replied. "I ran out of gas." As she went on to describe the incident, Powell realized that she had run out of gas less than half a mile from where he had sat fuming and immobilized in his car a few days earlier.

"What did you do after you ran out of gas?" Powell asked, intrigued by the similarities of their situations.

"I climbed down the hill on the west side of the freeway," she replied matter-of-factly.

Powell's eyebrows raised. "But there's a big fence at the bottom of that hill!" he said disbelievingly.

"Yes," said Mrs. Brady. "I climbed over it."

"Then what did you do?"

"I found a phone and called for help."

"That's incredible!" he whistled. "You must have felt really frustrated as you were going through all that."

"Oh, no!" she said with a laugh. "Actually, I felt exhilarated. It was a great adventure."

John Powell learned a big lesson about attitude that day. It's a lesson you and I need to grasp as well. When we stumble in life, or when something comes along and knocks us down, we need to make a choice—an attitude choice. It's our decision whether we will lay there in the dust, feeding on bitterness and self-pity, or pick ourselves up and go on. No matter what we have done, what others have done to us, or how hard our circumstances may be, there is one thing that cannot be taken from us: the ability to choose our attitude.

This truth was vividly demonstrated to me some years ago by my friend Stan Copeland. In the spring of 1965 Stan and I were members of a high school mile relay team which competed in the Iowa State Indoor Track Championships. Stan was the starting runner of our four-man team and I ran the final quarter-mile leg of the relay.

It was time for our race and I watched anxiously as Stan settled into the starting blocks with the baton in his right hand. The gun sounded and Stan shot out of the blocks. He had taken only a few strides when the runner in the next lane accidentally bumped Stan, knocking his glasses and our baton to the track. Staggering to maintain his balance, Stan bent low and scooped up the glasses and baton. Looking down the track, he saw that he was already 60 yards behind the pack. At that point in the race, Stan had to make an instant attitude choice: give up or go on. Many runners would have quit and no one would have blamed them. But Stan was there to run and nothing was going to knock him out of that race.

The crowd began to cheer as Stan kicked into gear and ran the fastest 440 yards of his career. Our baton was passed to the second runner, then to the third, and finally to me. Inspired by Stan's courageous example, each of us gave his very best effort and each of us ran his very best race. We didn't win, but we finished second—only 1.7 seconds behind the winners. We had no gold medal or state championship, but we all felt we had won a victory of courage and a victory of attitude.

Later that evening the four of us were eating in a restaurant when we were approached by the track coach of another school. He was one of the best known and most respected coaches in the state. Looking at all of us, but especially at Stan, he said, "I've been coaching track for over 30 years and that was the most courageous race I've ever seen a team run."

When you stumble, attitude is the key to picking yourself up and getting back into the race. You *can* say with Paul in 2 Timothy 4:7-8, "I have fought the good fight, I have finished the race, I have kept the faith. Now there is in store for me the crown of righteousness, which the Lord, the righteous Judge, will award to me on that day."

7

The Hands of a Servant

The name Linda Marchiano probably doesn't mean much to you. Linda Marchiano is a servant of others. She is a lonely crusader in a battle against some of the most powerful, predatory, and well-financed forces in our society: the pornography industry. In her quiet and unassuming way, this courageous young mother of two has carried the fight against pornography from her suburban Long Island home all the way to the United States Senate. She has given authoritative testimony about pornography's destructive effect both on those who view it and those who perform in it. A leading spokeswoman for Women Against Pornography, Mrs. Marchiano has written two major books attacking the pornography trade.

Though the name Linda Marchiano is hardly a household word, her credentials as an authority on pornography are unimpeachable. For the world has also known Linda Marchiano by another name, the name "Linda Lovelace," star of the notorious X-rated film *Deep Throat*. The film cost a mere $22,000 to produce, yet grossed more money at the box office than *Star Wars*.

Today Linda Marchiano seeks to make society aware of her story—a story which is repeated thousands of times in the lives of other women. For even though pornography is often called a "victimless crime" or a "harmless fantasy," Linda Marchiano reveals that she *was* an exploited victim. As the "star" of *Deep Throat*, she was drugged, beaten, and forced to perform for the camera acts she found revolting even in private.

Linda Marchiano understands something we all need to learn. An essential key to overcoming the pain of the past is becoming involved in service to others. By squarely facing our hurt and using it to bring healing to others, we can actually transform that hurt into something beautiful. Linda Marchiano is courageously utilizing the pain of her past to divert untold thousands of young women—and even children—from the kind of ordeal she experienced. After all, who is better qualified to warn our society about the pernicious nature of pornography than someone who was inside the industry and experienced its evils firsthand?

Similarly, who is better qualified to reach out to alcoholics or drug addicts than a recovered alcoholic or addict? Who is better qualified to reach out to the jobless than someone who has conquered his own trial of unemployment? When we are able to transform our pain into service to others, we have captured the deepest essence of what it means to be a Christian, a follower and imitator of Jesus Christ.

I can think of no more succinct description of the Christian life than the word *servanthood*. First, we are called to serve God and His Son Jesus. Romans 12:11 encourages us to "keep your spiritual fervor, serving the Lord." Colossians 3:24 tells us, "It is the Lord Jesus Christ you are serving." In John 12:26, Jesus says, "Whoever serves me must follow me; and where I am, my servant also will be. My Father will honor the one who serves me." And Matthew 25:21 contains the welcome we look forward to hearing from our Lord: "Well done, good and faithful servant!... Come and share your master's happiness!"

Second, we are to be servants of others. In 1 Corinthians 16:15, Paul commends those who devote themselves "to the service of the saints." In Galatians 5:13, the apostle says, "Serve one another in love." In Ephesians 4:11-12, Paul says that Christ gave apostles, prophets, evangelists, pastors, and teachers "to prepare God's people for works of service." And 1 Peter 4:10 tells us, "Each one should use whatever gift he has received to serve others, faithfully administering God's grace in its various forms."

Romans 8:29 reveals that God wants us to become like Christ. And as we study the life of Christ in order to better imitate his life, we see that the example he gave to us was that of a servant. In Matthew 20:28, Jesus said of himself, "The Son of Man did not come to be served, but to serve." Philippians 2:5-7 encourages us to have the same attitude as Jesus Christ who, even though he was God in the flesh, made himself of no importance, "taking the very nature of a servant."

In John 13:1-17 Jesus left us a vivid example of servanthood. During the Last Supper, Jesus wrapped a towel around his waist and poured water into a basin. Then he went from disciple to disciple, washing and drying each man's feet.

When he came to Peter, his impetuous friend was too proud to be served by Jesus. " 'No,' said Peter, 'you shall never wash my feet.'

"Jesus answered, 'Unless I wash you, you have no part with me.' "

So Jesus washed the feet of all his disciples, including proud Peter. When he finished, Jesus asked, "Do you understand what I have done for you? . . . Now that I, your Lord and Teacher, have washed your feet, you also should wash one another's feet. I have set you an example that you should do as I have done for you."

Jesus taught his disciples—and us—how to stoop to greatness. His disciples had proud hearts and so do we. And people with proud hearts have dirty feet. Jesus taught us that servanthood—getting our own hands dirty as we cleanse the feet of others—is the essence of the Christian life. And by his example, he showed us what true Christian servanthood is like.

First, Jesus showed us that a servant must be willing to be served. At first Peter would not allow the Lord to wash his feet. It might seem that Peter responded out of humility, as if saying he was unworthy to have his feet washed by Jesus. But the literal translation of Peter's words reveals his pride and unwillingness to be served: "No, you shall never wash my feet until eternity!" But Jesus patiently explained to Peter that the person who is too proud to *be served* is unqualified to *serve*.

This is a lesson you may need to learn during your pilgrimage to a new beginning. Perhaps you, like Peter, are reluctant to receive service from others. You may say, "No, you shall never help me with my problems! You shall never hear me cry out in my pain! No matter how bad things get, I will rely on myself!" That's the voice of pride, not the voice of a servant. Like Peter, we find it hard to admit we have dirty feet. But we cannot begin to find cleansing and wholeness until we admit our need. Though a servant must be willing to give, he cannot be too proud to receive.

Second, Jesus showed us that a servant is not selective. Jesus washed the feet of *all* his disciples—including Judas, his betrayer. There are some people we serve happily and easily. We don't mind being servants to those who look like us, think like us, dress as we dress, and support a similar lifestyle. But are we willing to wash the feet of a skid-row drunk, a lonely old woman in a rest home, or a victim of AIDS forgotten and dying in an inner-city hospital? A proud heart is selective, but a serving heart makes no distinctions.

I struggle every day with these principles. I struggle with the choice between serving as Christ served or "serving" selectively, pridefully, and selfishly. Recently my two children and I accompanied 50 young people from my church on an outreach mission to an extremely poor community in

Mexico. My son Nathan, who was then eight years old, befriended several Mexican boys in the town. Two of them,
Felipe and Sergio, were especially friendly to Nathan, and
the three boys enjoyed playing soccer together. I enjoyed
being with Felipe and Sergio too, and I wanted to be a servant
to them. I wanted to care for their physical and spiritual
needs and to find some way to help them out of their poverty.
The desire to wash the feet of Felipe and Sergio came easily
and naturally.

But there was another boy in the village named Oscar. He
was the same age as Felipe and Sergio, but he was a tough
kid—sullen and withdrawn. He wasn't very friendly to Nathan. And I didn't feel like being a servant to Oscar. I didn't
want to wash his feet.

But the voice of Jesus broke through the sinfulness and
selfishness of my heart that week. He said to me, "I washed
the feet of every man in the upper room, Ron. I even washed
the feet of Judas. I know it's easy to be a servant to Felipe and
Sergio—but I want you to be a servant to Oscar too. Try to
look beyond that little boy's hard exterior and see the hurt in
his heart."

I didn't see a dramatic change in Oscar during the week I
was in that dusty Mexican village. But I did notice a small
change occurring in my own heart. I found myself becoming
a little more like a servant—and a little more like Christ.

Servanthood transforms lives. Servanthood produces joy.
Servanthood opens the door to a new beginning.

Linda Marchiano made the courageous choice to confront
her past rather than run from it. She lives daily with the
knowledge that *Deep Throat*—which she considers to be a
film record of an act of rape—continues to play in theaters
and on videocassette recorders across the country. Though
she has been attacked by critics, threatened by elements of
organized crime, and plagued by serious health problems in
recent years, she continues her courageous fight against
pornography. She continues to transform her pain into service to the men, women, and children who are being—or may

one day be—exploited by this predatory evil. Today she says, "The bad experiences I had to go through have value, and a life that once had no meaning now has some meaning."[1] Linda Marchiano has triumphed over her past because she has become a servant of others.

May it be so with you and me. A.W. Tozer observed that the only way *up* in the Christian life is *down*. If we want to rise up in triumph over the failures and hurts of the past, we need to go down on our knees as servants. We must become servants of God and servants of one another.

But I need to give you a cautionary word about *priorities* in servanthood. You may think you are already a servant because you are spending your prime time, your spare time, and your nights for the sake of others. Yet you may set yourself up for a tragic failure if you neglect to prioritize wisely your service to God and others. I've known people who worked themselves into exhaustion serving their churches or civic groups. In seeking to serve others so tirelessly, they do a catastrophic *dis*service to their families.

One such person was a Youth For Christ leader in his mid-thirties named Fred. I met Fred at a youth workers' convention in Dallas a few years ago. He approached me after a presentation I made on the subject of priorities for Christian servants. "Your talk hit me right between the eyes," he said. "Ron, I've been away from my family for about 300 nights in the last year. Lately I've been having a lot of trouble with my teenaged son. He's sullen, rebellious, and he's getting involved with the wrong kind of friends and activities."

Seated nearby, and listening intently as Fred and I talked, was my good friend Bill LeTourneau, an executive director with YFC and a model servant. Bill, his wife Julie, and I traveled together from California to the convention. During the trip to Dallas, one leg of our flight was cancelled and we were bumped to another flight. So each of us was compensated with a free round-trip ticket to any destination served by the airline. Bill and Julie were excited because the free tickets suddenly made possible their dream vacation to New York.

After hearing Fred's story, Bill had a talk with Julie and then took Fred aside. "My wife and I want you to have these," Bill said as he pressed the couple's airline tickets into Fred's hand. "We want you and your son to enjoy a free trip to somewhere special and spend at least a week with each other."

Fred was flabbergasted. And I was blessed. Bill and Julie postponed their vacation for the sake of someone they barely knew. That's servanthood! At the same time Fred learned that serving other people's kids means little if his own son is neglected. To be God's kind of servant means being a servant to one's family first. Servanthood begins at home.

We can learn a lot about servanthood from children. Chad Thompson was only seven years old, but he understood and lived out the true meaning of Christlike servanthood.

A shy, reserved little boy, Chad had very few friends in his second-grade class. But on one cold day in January, Chad came home from school with an idea, a dream. He decided that he would make personalized valentines for each of the children in his class. When Chad told his mother about his idea, she sighed and grieved for him inwardly. Day after day she had watched Chad walk home from school alone, usually about a block behind a group of laughing, skipping children who had excluded him. Now he was setting himself up for further disappointment by making valentines for children who would not return his gesture of friendship.

But Chad was determined. Every night for three weeks Chad carefully cut out paper hearts and painstakingly scrawled crayon messages. Finally he had a stack of 35 hand-made valentines, one for each member of his class.

On the morning of February 14th, Chad left for school with a heart full of excitement and anticipation, and a paper sack full of friendship messages for his classmates. His mother watched from the door until he disappeared down the street.

Then she went to the kitchen to bake cookies. *Perhaps a plate of cookies will ease Chad's disappointment,* she thought, *if he comes home this afternoon without a valentine of his own.*

Afternoon came and the milk and cookies were waiting on the table. Chad's mother went to the window when she heard the familiar sound of second-graders walking home from school. First came the group walking playfully together. And then came Chad, alone as usual, his empty hands stuffed into his pockets.

Chad's mother met him at the door with a hug. "Not a one, Mom," he said, looking up at her. "Not a single one." His mother's heart was broken for her empty-handed son and she began to cry. But she didn't understand what her little seven-year-old servant meant. "Not a one," Chad continued. "I didn't forget a single one! I remembered to give a valentine to every boy and girl in my class."

This is what the life of a servant is like—thinking of others rather than self. A servant gives without thought for repayment. A servant loves without discrimination, and even in the face of rejection. A servant turns his own hurt into grace toward others.

There is pain in your past, but there can be joy in your future. Whatever your hurt may be, understand that nothing happens to you without a purpose. Everything we endure prepares us to be better servants to God and others, and to make us more like Christ.

These lines by an anonymous poet describe the emptying process we go through on the road to becoming servants:

> One by one, he took from me
> All the things I valued most,
> Until I was left empty-handed.
> Every glittering toy was lost.
> And I walked earth's highway grieving
> In my rags and poverty.
> Till I heard his voice inviting

"Lift those empty hands to me!"
Then I turned my hands toward heaven
And he filled them with a store
Of his own transcendent riches,
Till they could contain no more.
And at last I comprehended,
With my simple mind and dull,
That God cannot pour his riches
Into hands already full.

Look at your hands right now and ask yourself, "Are these the hands of a servant?"

8

How Well Do You Know Your Father?

Out on the lake in upstate New York, a boat capsized. People began shouting. "Someone please help us! He can't swim!"

On the boat landing stood a seventeen-year-old boy. Just a few feet from him, a boat was tied up, a pair of oars resting in the hull. Though a strong rower and an expert swimmer, the boy looked on from the landing, unmoving. Then he turned and looked pleadingly up the hill toward his house. His father was sitting in the porch swing, staring out toward the lake.

"They said a man's drowning out there!" shouted the boy. His father said nothing. The boy waited a long time, and then he said again, "He's drowning out there!" He bent toward the mooring line.

"Shut up!" snapped the boy's father, "and don't you ever touch that boat without my permission!"

Helpless to move, with an obedience ensured by seventeen years of physical and verbal punishment, the boy stood on the landing. It was a few minutes before other boats began to converge on the scene of the accident. A few minutes more, and a man was pulled out of the water—dead.

I might have saved him, thought the boy, angry and a-shamed. And from that day forward, he vowed that he would never again allow his conscience to be overridden by his father's cruel dictates—and this father's grip on his son was forever broken.

Though submerged and suppressed, the horror of that day, together with the feelings of anger and shame, would remain with him for many years to come. Here was a young man with a deep need for a new beginning—the opportunity to right an unrightable wrong. It would seem almost impossible to even hope for—but one day, many years later, he would get that new beginning . . .

Fathers have a special responsibility for the shaping of the lives and attitudes of their children. In particular, fathers play an essential role in shaping a child's image of God. A distant, uninvolved father frequently builds in his children the idea that their Heavenly Father is a remote and impersonal deity somewhere in the silent cosmos. Children of an angry, vindictive father often grow to fear the capricious judgment of an angry God. Children of a demanding father often grow up feeling inadequate and insecure, as if they will never quite measure up in the eyes of God.

Because the father is the model for the son, there has lately been an increasing amount of attention focused on father-son relationships in books and television and radio talk-shows. What is equally important but much less understood in our society today is the crucial importance of father-*daughter* relationships. Noted author-psychologist Ross Campbell strongly emphasizes the need daughters have to receive attention from their fathers in the form of unconditional love, eye contact, focused attention, and an affirming touch or hug—a need which begins as early as age two and peaks in most girls at the critical stage of eleven to thirteen years old.

There was one father who—because of some deep hurts he had suffered in his own childhood—was incapable of giving to his daughter the kind of emotional nurturing Dr. Campbell describes. This father never told his daughter he loved her, and never went to her plays, recitals, or graduation exercises as she was growing up. Throughout their relationship and well into her adulthood, he was a cold, unfeeling figure at the edge of her life—and at the center of her pain. He was a religious man, but his religion seemed to express itself only in harsh judgment and criticism, never in grace or acceptance. They continued to clash bitterly, even after she had become a woman in her forties with grown children of her own.

It was out of this pain that she wrote to a Christian psychologist and poured out her despair. The psychologist wrote back and replied,

> Many of us spend a great deal of energy in the search for those things we could never attain in childhood—love, acceptance, security, contentment. Even though your father has never satisfied these emotional needs in your life, you still hope you can somehow gain his approval. It is that forlorn hope that he will somehow change into the father you've always wanted that gives him the power to hurt you again and again. I think he will probably continue to hurt you until you accept the fact that he is simply *unable* to change. It is as though he has a permanent handicap. He is "blind," so to speak, to your emotional needs. It is an emotional blindness that was probably inflicted upon him by some painful event in his own childhood. As you learn to see him as a man with hurts and handicaps of his own, I believe you will begin to find healing from the hurt of his rejection.

The first time she read this letter was a transforming moment in the life of this hurting daughter of an unfeeling father. From then on, she began to grow in the knowledge that—however she had been rejected by her earthly father—she was the daughter of a loving heavenly Father, a Father who truly demonstrates his love to us and accepts us exactly as we are.

This kind of loving, accepting, affirming Father is pictured for us in the parable Jesus tells in Luke 15. Though this story has come to be called the Parable of the Prodigal Son, it seems to me that the central point of this story is not so much about the son as about the *father*—this loving, accepting father whom Jesus presents to us as his portrait of that best of all fathers, the God of a new beginning.

You probably know the story. A father has amassed a fortune and had arranged to leave it to his two sons. He was a very good father to his boys, providing positive leadership in his home. The elder son had served his father faithfully for years, and had not disobeyed a single one of his father's commands. And the younger son, though he displayed less appreciation for his dad's love, clearly demonstrated that he had a very open relationship with his father. He approached his father boldly and said, in effect, "Dad, I'm ready to go my own way. Just give me my share of the inheritance, and I'll be shoving off." There's no hint here that he was intimidated by a cold or distant father; rather, this son clearly saw his father as approachable.

This father responded by talking the matter over calmly with his son.

"Very well," he concluded. "Here's your half of the inheritance, son. Go in peace." This boy, who has sometimes been pictured as a runaway, was actually given his freedom by this patient, understanding father.

So the younger son set off on his own to live a life of open debauchery. This is the part of the story people seem most familiar with—possibly because so many Christians over the years have dwelt on all the sin this boy committed, and all the woes that follow as a result. But again, I think the real focus of this story is the *father*.

What did he do while his son was away? Did he write off his son as worthless? Did he grumble, "So that's the thanks I get for all the years I poured into that ungrateful boy!'"? Did he wring his hands in anxiety and guilt, wondering, "If only I had disciplined more firmly—If only I had spent more time with my boy—If only I had prayed more faithfully—Then my boy wouldn't have left home!'"? No, he did none of those things. Instead, he simply waited—and trusted. He was calmly and serenely confident that his Heavenly Father would do what he, an earthly father, could not do: *change his boy's heart.* And he was ready—*always* ready—to give his son a new beginning.

One day the son *did* return—hungry, penniless, humiliated, remorseful. He no longer regarded himself as a son, but was willing to simply labor for his father as a servant. And when this son made the decision to return home, he was not returning to the farm, to his room, to his possessions or to a comfortable way of life. No, *he was returning to his father!* He said, "I will arise and go back to my father." It was this loving father himself who was the magnet for this wayward boy, drawing him home.

Here we learn something significant about the father: As the boy approached, the father saw his son far in the distance. Do you suppose this father just happened to glance toward the road as his son approached? I doubt it. I think Jesus is telling us that this father rose early each morning and went out on a hill and daily searched the horizon for his missing son. And every time he saw a silhouette on the road, he hoped and prayed that it was his boy.

When I think of the ardent love this father had for his boy, I am reminded of the father who followed the evangelistic campaigns of Dwight L. Moody late in the last century. In city after city, at the end of each meeting, he asked Moody's permission to stand on the platform and address the audience. He stood before the congregation in a rumpled suit—an elderly gentleman with thin white hair and desolate eyes—

and he looked out over the crowd and said, "Is my son George here? George, are you here? George, if you are here, please come talk to me. I love you, George, and I can't die at peace until we have reconciled." Each time he made his announcement, there was silence in the audience. Then, sadly, the man would sit down.

One night, there came a knock on the door of Moody's hotel room. He opened the door to find a stranger. "Mr. Moody," said the stranger, "I want you to tell that man to stop making a fool of himself on that platform."

"You mean the elderly man who is seeking his son George?" asked Moody. "Why, what possible interest do you have in this matter?"

"My name is George," he answered. "That man is my father."

"Then why don't you go to him and reconcile with him? Surely you can see that he loves you very much."

"His love means nothing to me," said the son. "He's an embarrassment to me, and I just want him to go home and leave me alone."

And even though Moody continued to plead with the young man, history contains no record that this son ever made peace with his father. Happily, the story Jesus told in Luke 15 has a much different ending. For when the loving father of Jesus' story finally saw his boy returning, this loving father *ran* to meet the boy, and he hugged him and kissed him.

This father didn't demand an apology or an explanation— nor did he even wait for the son to speak! For all he knew, his son might have been unrepentant, and was simply returning to demand more cash to finance his hedonistic lifestyle. But this father was moved with compassion and unconditional love. The boy had carefully rehearsed a speech for that meeting—"Father, I've sinned against heaven and before you. I'm no longer worthy to be your son . . ."—but I doubt he was able to finish even the first few words before being smothered by the embrace of his father.

Instead of blame, this father showered his son with forgiveness! Instead of rejection, he lavished unconditional
acceptance on his boy! He didn't even put his son on proba-
tion. "Quick!" he shouted to his servants. "Bring the robe of
honor! Get the ring for my son's finger! Give the farmhands
the day off and slay the calf we've been saving! We're going to
have a barbecue in my son's honor!"

And that, Jesus tells us in this parable, is the kind of
Heavenly Father we have. His business is forgiveness, not
blame; healing, not inflicting hurt; accepting, not casting
aside. The reason Jesus told this story is that he wants you
and me to know exactly what kind of Father we have. He
wants us to know that *God's greatest delight* is to transform
our sin and failure into *a new beginning*.

A new beginning. That was what George Orick needed.
Orick was the man who, as a seventeen-year-old boy, had
watched from a boat landing while another man drowned.

It was 41 years later, in the remote frozen wastes of Antarctica, that Orick got the new beginning he needed. It was
December 1982. Orick was part of a camera crew that accompanied Hugh Downs to Antarctica's Ross Ice Shelf on a film
assignment for the ABC News *20/20* program. He had just
finished filming a brief segment with Downs, and was walking alongside a crevasse. Suddenly one of Orick's companions, Frank Williamson, a scientist with the research project
that the ABC News team was visiting, broke through the
treacherous snow crust and slipped into the three-foot-wide
crevasse. Williamson was clutching the edge of the crevasse
with one hand, tenuously suspended over the icy maw of
death.

Instantly, Orick threw himself upon the scientist's hand
and anchored it in the snow with the full weight of his body.
He had landed fully six feet from where he had been standing. Had his heroic leap been a few inches longer he might
have tumbled into the crevasse as well.

Hugh Downs threw himself alongside Orick and gripped the dangling man by the shoulder of his parka. Soon other scientists and news crewmen scrambled over to help. Ultimately it took a dozen people to haul Williamson out—but it was the daring split-second action of one man, George Orick, that gave him his chance to live.

Shortly after the incident, Orick reflected in a magazine article on the two life-and-death decisions he had made—one as a young man of seventeen, and the much different decision he had made on an ice shelf at the bottom of the world. "Would that man in the lake have lived had I defied my father?" he wondered, though he would never truly know the answer. "We don't give up our guilt easily; we have to be sure. I inspected and re-inspected both events, and always the same answer: I did not give the drowning man a chance; I did give Frank a chance. No question: I had been given a second chance—an opportunity to right a terrible wrong."[1]

That is how our Heavenly Father is at work in our lives— whether in such life-and-death situations as George Orick experienced or in the little details of our everyday affairs. He is the God of a second chance, the God of a new beginning. Now the question that confronts us is, "How well do you know your Heavenly Father?"

This is a question which brings to mind the story of the young boy who burst into the great throne chamber of a medieval king. The boy was skipping and singing as children do, completely oblivious to the regal sobriety of his surroundings. Suddenly he was intercepted by an armored soldier, who grasped the boy by the arm. "Have you no respect, lad?" hissed the soldier. "Don't you know that the man on the throne is your *king*?"

The boy wriggled out of the soldier's grasp and danced away, laughing. "He is *your* king!" the boy called back. "But he is *my father*!" And the boy bounced up to the dais and leaped into the king's lap, where he received the proud embrace and fond kiss of his loving father.

How well do you know *your* Father in heaven? If the image you have of God is that of a distant and silent cosmic deity or an angry tyrant, then I invite you to meet *my* Heavenly Father, the kind of father described by Jesus in Luke 15. He is the God of grace, the God of forgiveness—the God of a new beginning. He is a loving father who eagerly scans the horizon, searching for his errant children who are looking for their home.

If you are looking for a new beginning in life, then come home to your Heavenly Father. Let him receive you, embrace you, and robe you in honor. And then begin building that deep and abiding quality of relationship with him that will enable you to say with confidence as you walk with him through this life, "Yes, I know him well. I know his will, I know his heart. I know I can trust his love for me because he's my Father!"

9

The Threshold of a New Life

Frederick Charrington was a member of the wealthy family in England which owned the Charrington Brewery. His personal fortune, derived solely from his brewing enterprise, exceeded $6 million.

One night, Charrington was walking along a London street with a few friends. Suddenly the door of a pub flew open just a few steps ahead of the group, and a man staggered out into the street with a woman clinging desperately to him. The man, obviously very drunk, was swearing at the woman and trying to push her away. The woman was gaunt and clad in rags. She sobbed and pleaded with the drunken man, who was her husband.

"Please, dear, please!" she cried as Charrington and his friends watched. "The children haven't eaten in two days! And I've not eaten in a week! For the love of God, please come home! Or if you must stay, just give me a few coins so I can buy the children some—"

Her pleas were brutally cut off as her husband struck her a savage blow. She collapsed to the stone pavement like a rag doll. The man stood over her with his fists clenched, poised as if to strike her again. Charrington leaped forward and grasped him. The man struggled, swearing violently, but Charrington pinned the man's arms securely behind his back. Charrington's companions rushed to the woman's side and began ministering to her wounds. A short time later a policeman led the drunken man away and the woman was taken to a nearby hospital.

As Charrington brushed himself off, he noticed a lighted sign in the window of the pub: "Drink Charrington Ale." The multi-millionaire brewer was suddenly shaken to the core of his being. He realized that his confrontation with the violent husband would not have happened if the man's brain had not been awash with the Charrington family's product. "When I saw that sign," he later wrote, "I was stricken just as surely as Paul on the Damascus Road. Here was the source of my family wealth, and it was producing untold human misery before my own eyes. Then and there I pledged to God that not another penny of that money should come to me."

History records that Frederick Charrington became one of the most well-known temperance activists in England. He renounced his share of the family fortune and devoted the rest of his life to the ministry of freeing men and women from the curse of alcoholism.

Frederick Charrington was a man whose life exemplified the word *repentance*. Repentance—the course of Charrington's life was dramatically turned around. Repentance—he made a total break with his former life and allowed God to create for him a totally new life with new meaning and purpose. Repentance—he disposed of his fortune, convicted that what once was a profit had become a spiritual liability.

Repentance is the means by which we, like Frederick Charrington, appropriate the grace of the God of a new beginning. It is the means by which we break with the dead past and find the total newness of life that God offers us.

True, life-changing repentance is made up of several components. First, repentance begins with self-examination. We start by honestly measuring ourselves against the standard of God's commands in Scripture. At the same time, we must stop measuring ourselves against other people or the standards of our culture. As we study the Scriptures and come to an ever deeper understanding of the guidelines God gives us in his word, his Spirit will bring increasingly greater conviction of sin in our lives.

I find that the end of the day, just before I go to sleep, is a good time to replay the events of the day in my mind. When the world is very quiet, I examine my day—what I've thought, said, done, and ought to have done. As I review my activities, the Spirit of God often brings to my mind areas of sin and failure, as well as the joys and accomplishments of the day just spent.

Second, when we experience sorrow over the sin we have discovered within ourselves, we then express our confession to God in prayer. We confess our sins specifically and concretely. Does that mean that we must confess every individual sin we've ever committed in order to be forgiven? Obviously that's not even possible. God never intended us to live in fear that we forgot to cross a *t* or dot an *i* somewhere along the line. He's not looking for perfectly itemized confessions. All God requires is that we are honest with ourselves and with him. As 1 John 1:9 tells us, "If we confess our sins,"—those specific sins that the Holy Spirit brings to our minds—"he is faithful and just and will forgive us our sins and purify us from all unrighteousness." As we confess our individual sins, God purifies us of *all* sin—even those sins we've forgotten.

The third component of repentance is acceptance of God's forgiveness. If you have confessed your sin, you must recognize that God has forgiven you. Accept the clean slate God gives you. Then move ahead boldly to live as a forgiven child of God. If you are tempted to harbor the guilt of the past, remember that it is not the God of a new beginning who is accusing you. Rather, guilt over already confessed sin comes straight from the evil god of this age, Satan the Accuser. Throw off those accusations and your regrets from the past. You have confessed your sin and you are now forgiven. You can forgive yourself. You are free.

The final step of repentance is commitment to a repentant life-style. When we receive God's forgiveness, we must give ourselves to a life-style which reflects our new direction. We must not turn back or even glance back.

As a young man, St. Augustine felt the call of God upon his life. Yet he was not quite willing to make a complete break from his sins in order to follow God's call. As he struggled with God over who would control his life, Augustine prayed, "Lord, save me from my sins—but not quite yet." As his inner struggle continued, he eventually was able to pray, "Lord, save me from all my sins—except one." He had edged closer to God, but he still shielded one area of his life from God's control. At last his struggle with God led him to pray, "Lord, save me from *all* my sins and save me *now*!" No longer caught in a miserable struggle that fragmented his soul, Augustine finally found complete joy and peace. The war was over when he made a total commitment of himself to God.

Sadly, there are Christians who use the forgiveness of God as an excuse to continue sinning. Such people do not truly understand repentance, forgiveness, or the grace of God. They practice what Dietrich Bonhoeffer called "cheap grace." In *The Cost of Discipleship*, Bonhoeffer wrote:

> Cheap grace is the deadly enemy of our Church....
> Cheap grace means grace as a doctrine, a principle, a system. It means forgiveness of sins proclaimed as a general truth, the love of God taught as the Christian "conception" of God. An intellectual assent to that idea is held to be of itself sufficient to secure remission of sins.... Cheap grace is not the kind of forgiveness of sin which frees us from the toils of sin. Cheap grace is the grace we bestow on ourselves....

Costly grace is the gospel which must be *sought* again and again, the gift which must be *asked* for, the door at which a man must *knock*. Such grace is *costly* because it calls us to follow, and it is *grace* because it calls us to follow *Jesus Christ*. It is costly because it costs a man his life, and it is grace because it gives a man the only true life. It is costly because it condemns sin, and grace because it justifies the sinner. Above all, it is *costly* because it cost God the life of his Son: "ye were bought at a price," and what has cost God much cannot be cheap for us.[1]

This is exactly the point Paul makes in Romans 6:1-2: "What shall we say, then? Shall we go on sinning so that grace may increase? By no means! We died to sin; how can we live in it any longer?" And in verse 11 he concludes, "Count yourselves dead to sin but alive to God in Christ Jesus."

Living a life-style of repentance means that if there is anything in our lives that might tempt us to turn back to our old sins, we will dispose of it or destroy it. If there is a niggling little reservation in the corner of my mind which says, "I can still return to this sin every once in awhile," I will immediately say, "No! By God's grace and with his help I am finished with this sin now and forever!"

We will stumble and we will fail. But the repentant life-style will call us back to self-examination, confession, and a new commitment to following Christ. We will no longer see sin as a normal part of our lives, but as a deviation from the new, forgiven life-style we have chosen. And as we commit ourselves to repentance, we may need to take the added step of asking a trusted Christian brother or sister to hold us accountable for our life-style. When we invite another person to watch us, to check on our progress, to question us, and to challenge us when we fail, we visibly demonstrate the earnestness of our commitment to Christ.

Repentance takes place when we see God for who he is and see ourselves for who we are. Repentance is a result of experiencing God's goodness, hearing God's Word, and being moved by God's Spirit. And one of the hard truths of life is that our deepest experiences of God's goodness sometimes come to us through painful trials such as loss, illness, depression, failure, or mistreatment.

The story of Job illustrates how God uses our trials to bring us to repentance and a closer relationship with himself. You are probably familiar with the intense suffering Job experienced as he lost his health, his possessions, and his loved ones. More than 40 chapters of the book of Job record his dialogue with God and others about his suffering. According to Job 42:5-6, Job finally came to a place of accepting his trial—a place of repentance: "My ears had heard of you," Job says to God of the time before his trial when he was healthy and prosperous, "but now my eyes have seen you. Therefore I ... repent in dust and ashes."

You may wonder what Job is repenting of. If ever there was a godly, righteous man, it was Job! He is the one of whom God says in Job 1:8: "There is no one on earth like him; he is blameless and upright, a man who fears God and shuns evil." Why must a blameless man repent?

I believe Job repented because his trial enabled him to see both God and himself with greater clarity. Repentance, remember, takes place when we see God for who he is and ourselves for who we are. Before his time of testing, Job *heard* of God. He had a head-knowledge of God, he had read the Scriptures, and he had good doctrine and theology. But through his suffering Job gained a face-to-face *experience* of God. In the laboratory of life, Job experienced God in such a way that he could say, "Now my eyes have seen you."

Because of this first-hand experience of God, Job said, "I repent." His vision of God had been expanded and his view of himself was reduced to a realistic scale. During his trial, the props had been knocked out from under his self-assurance, self-righteousness, and self-importance. At the same time, God revealed himself to Job in a powerful way, displaying his might, goodness, and holiness. Job was a righteous man by human standards, but he fell far short of God's standard of moral perfection. If a righteous man like Job saw a need for repentance, how much more do you and I need to exercise repentance?

A close friend of mine is the pastor of a large church in the San Francisco Bay area. A few years ago, a youth worker in his congregation was found to be practicing very serious sexual sin. The man had been a Christian for several years and was an outspoken witness for Christ. In fact, he had written a widely distributed booklet detailing his dramatic conversion to Christ. Yet his sinful life-style brought his testimony into disrepute.

So the elders of the church searched the Scriptures for guidance for confronting their erring brother about his sin and guiding him back to a life-style of obedience. In a very caring but straightforward way, the elders met with him, discussed his life-style, opened the Scriptures and prayed with him, and appealed to him to repent. But the man chose to continue in his pattern of sin.

With deep reluctance and sadness, the elders then exercised church discipline in accordance with principles found in such passages as Matthew 18 and 1 Corinthians 5. They were not only concerned for the spiritual welfare of the brother in sin, but for others in the church who could be affected by his sin. The elders barred him from the fellowship of the church while promising immediate restoration upon evidence of his repentance.

The erring brother remained out of fellowship of that church and all other churches for five years. His self-imposed exile was marked by bitterness and depression, and punctuated by periodic bouts with alcoholism. It was the pain of this black period in his life that ultimately drove him back to God and to the church. As one of the steps of his repentance, he sent a letter to my friend, the pastor of the church, asking that it be read to the congregation. The letter read, in part:

> My Fellow Christians,
>
> Several years ago the elders of our congregation held me accountable in accordance with Matthew 18:15-20. The charges against me were completely true. I cannot reverse history and undo the events which led to my downfall. I have harmed people and brought heartache to myself.
>
> After I became a Christian some 18 years ago, I failed to deal thoroughly with lust, covetousness, and immorality. In time I became self-deceived, proud, and arrogant. I am in need of your prayers and of your forgiveness for I have wronged you all.
>
> It is impossible for me to retrace my footsteps and right every wrong. However, I welcome the opportunity to meet and pray with anyone who has something against me that needs resolution. I am awaiting further grace and mercy from God in this matter and I now know that your actions were done in love for my own good and for the good of the body of Christ.

The letter provides a vivid glimpse into one man's repentant heart. His repentance issued into restoration, healing, and a new beginning.

The repentant brother was not merely *allowed* back into the fellowship of the church, he was *cheered* back into fellowship. A Sunday evening service was set aside for a special celebration full of symbols from the story of the prodigal son's return as described in Luke 15. Like the loving father in the story, this church honored its returning son. The pastor and elders placed a royal robe on the man's shoulders, slipped a ring on his finger, and put new shoes on his feet. They wept openly with the man as they embraced him. He once was lost, but now—by an act of repentance and the new-beginning grace of God—he was found. He was home.

God has done everything necessary for you and me to come home to a new beginning in life. He gives us grace, forgiveness, and strength to live each day as a new opportunity, full of possibility and adventure. But you and I must take this grace and appropriate it for our lives. We must receive the new life he offers us and live it with courage, zeal, and zest.

So the question that faces you and me as we stand on the threshold of this new beginning is, "Are you ready to break the chains of the past and step boldly into the future?" If you can answer "yes," you are ready to follow the steps of repentance: self-examination, confession, acceptance of forgiveness, and commitment. Until you make the decision to take these steps of repentance, the door to the new life God offers you is closed—not by God but by your unwillingness to step forward into the future.

The door to a new life is right in front of you. The key to that door is repentance. The choice to open the door and cross the threshold is yours. What will you decide?

10

The Fire Alarm

Jerry was a tall, strongly built, athletic young man. Yet in the month they had dated, Tricia found him to be as gentle as he was strong. She was pleased that Jerry didn't force his attentions on her as had some of the men she had dated. Jerry seemed genuinely interested in her as a person, not as a sexual conquest. And Tricia was falling in love.

One day the couple traveled to an isolated beach on the North Carolina shore. They sat close together on the beach, looking out over the Atlantic breakers and talking contentedly. Then Jerry began to caress Tricia romantically and unbutton her blouse. She gently pushed his hands away. Jerry immediately pulled back, tucked his chin between his knees, and wrapped himself in a sullen, wounded silence—a silence that lasted all the way home.

For several days afterward, Jerry was once again a perfect gentleman—considerate, complimentary, and solicitous of her needs. Nothing was ever said about the incident on the beach. But as they continued to date, Jerry persisted in making sexual advances, which Tricia gently refused. And each time she refused, Jerry acted hurt. "I didn't want to give him my body," she later recalled. "But the tension was agonizing. Somehow he made *me* feel guilty, as if *I* was the one hurting *him*."

One day they returned to their secluded spot on the North Carolina shore. Again Jerry made advances—but this time Tricia gave in. As soon as it was over, Tricia was enveloped in smothering guilt that clung to her and depressed her for weeks afterward. She couldn't understand it. Her friends seemed to enjoy flagrantly promiscuous life-styles without any apparent guilt. Yet Tricia was so miserable she took a trip to Pennsylvania just to escape her feelings. Upon returning home, she found this note:

> Tricia,
> It was nice knowing you. Too bad things didn't work out.
> >   Jerry

From then on, Jerry avoided her. Tricia later heard that Jerry began dating her because some of his friends bet him he couldn't "take" Tricia, the girl with the "straight" reputation. Whenever she saw any of Jerry's friends, she felt sick inside, certain that they knew everything that happened on the beach. She stopped dating altogether. She closed off her friendships. She tried to quench her feelings of guilt—but without success.

Tricia finally took her feelings to a Christian counselor. After hearing her story, he said, "Tricia, before you committed your life to Christ, you had good reason to feel guilty. Your guilt separated you from God. But the really liberating thing about being a Christian is that Jesus has dissolved all your guilt. That's why he died for you, Tricia—to wash away your sin."

Though she had been a Christian for several years, this was a new concept to Tricia. She viewed Christians as people who lived by a set of rules. When those rules were broken, the violator was supposed to feel guilty. The counselor assured Tricia that she could exchange her guilt for grace.

"I suggest," he continued, "that whenever the bad memories return, don't say, 'Oh, God, please forgive me.' Just say, 'I'm so thankful, God, that you've *already* forgiven me!'" And then he opened his Bible to 1 John 1:9 and showed it to her: "If we confess our sins, he is faithful and just and will forgive us our sins and purify us from all unrighteousness."

Today Tricia has that verse lettered on index cards which she keeps tacked to her bulletin board at home, clipped to her notebook, and taped to the dashboard of her car. "The memories occasionally return," she admits, "but each time they do I turn to God and thank him for forgiving me and making me pure in his eyes. It works: the guilt has disappeared."[1]

That's the liberating power of the God of a new beginning. We are not left to drown in our guilt. We are not forced to earn forgiveness under the lash of a whip. We do not need to excuse or rationalize our guilt. Instead, God empowers us to break the chains of our guilt. He gives us the courage to take an honest, clear-eyed look at ourselves and our sin—and then he shows us ourselves as he sees us. We are not perfect, but we are forgiven. By grace, God has washed away our sin because we have accepted the forgiveness Jesus purchased for us on the cross.

Obviously, our past does not magically disappear. Painful memories will recur. But as we grow in the knowledge of God's love for us, the sting of those memories will gradually be replaced by healing. Indeed, as the sting of guilt subsides, we will be able to recall the past with honesty and clarity, so we can learn not to repeat our mistakes. Even though the past is forgiven, we can learn from it to shape our future and to shape the person we are becoming.

Guilt comes to us in many forms. There is *false* guilt imposed on us by the expectations of those who attempt to manipulate us. This was the kind of guilt Jerry inflicted on Tricia early in their relationship. He made advances toward her, and when she resisted those advances he manipulated her by his sullen response so she actually felt guilty for doing what was right! This is the way false guilt works. When we understand that such guilt comes from a deceptive source, we can learn to avoid being tricked into even deeper guilt as Tricia was.

Then there is *burdensome* guilt, the second kind of guilt Tricia experienced. It's the kind we carry around on our backs like a weight because we have not learned to experience the liberation of God's grace. Burdensome guilt breaks down our self-image. Like false guilt, burdensome guilt also comes from a deceptive source—a deceptive *spiritual* source. Satan tries to rob us of the freedom we enjoy in God's grace by accusing us of sins which God has already forgiven, forgotten, and buried in the deepest sea.

Those who stagger under the weight of burdensome guilt actually experience a kind of inner divorce. One part of the self splits away, recoiling in disgust from its mirror image. As we are repeatedly hammered by the painful memories of past sins, our view of ourselves becomes fragmented. We begin to take on the mutually irreconcilable roles of prosecutor, defendant, judge, jury, and executioner. When we experience that feeling of inner fragmentation, we need to discover the reality of inner oneness by recognizing that in Christ we already have peace with our forgiving Father. Like Tricia, we need to keep the words of 1 John 1:9 on our mirror, on the refrigerator door, on the bed post, on the dashboard, and over the front door: "If we confess our sins, he is faithful and just and will forgive us our sins and purify us from all unrighteousness."

Hannah Whitall Smith was a Christian writer in the nineteenth century who had a passion for helping other Christians experience God's forgiveness. Once, after Hannah had finished a conference talk, a little girl about nine years old approached the platform and tugged on Hannah's dress. Hannah looked down at the child's inquisitive face. "Yes, little girl?" she asked, bending down.

"Does Jesus always forgive our sins as soon as we ask him?" the child asked.

"Of course he does," Hannah replied.

"*Just* as soon?" the girl pressed, lines of doubt creasing her forehead.

"Yes, dear. He forgives us the very moment we ask him."

"Well," the girl said deliberately, "I cannot believe Jesus forgives us so quickly. First I think he would want us to feel very sorry for two or three days. And then I think he would want us to ask his forgiveness a great many times. And we must ask him in very pretty words, too—not just in common talk. I believe this is the way Jesus forgives us, and you need not try to make me think he forgives me right at once—no matter what the Bible says!"

Hannah Smith later observed that the little girl had only said what most Christians think. And I have to concur: Time after time, I've seen Christians separate themselves from God more completely by their *remorse* and *guilt* than they ever did by their *sin*. Perhaps we think it is presumptuous and irreverent to expect immediate forgiveness from God as if it were our due. Perhaps we think we must personally atone for our sins or pay for them in some way. We feel we should suffer, pay a price, or ask God's forgiveness a great many times and in just the right words—and then maybe he will forgive us.

That's the deception of burdensome guilt. It robs us of our sense of self-worth and our sense of position as children of a loving God. Burdensome guilt paralyzes us; but the grace of God liberates us. We cannot pay for our sin. If we could, Christ died in vain. Christ alone has paid the price for our sin. We are saved from sin and guilt by grace through faith. God's forgiveness is free and abundant; there are no strings attached.

There is a third kind of guilt—*authentic* guilt. Authentic guilt does not come from a deceptive source, but directly from the Holy Spirit. In the Bible it is called "the conviction of sin," and it has a very specific and short-term purpose. Authentic guilt does not linger beyond the point of forgiveness. It does not drive us to despair. It does not make us feel worthless. It does not paralyze us. On the contrary, authentic guilt spurs us to positive action.

Authentic guilt is like a fire alarm. When we sin, our conscience sounds a warning, a call to action. When the alarm of guilt sounds, it's time to act. It's time to deal with the very real danger of sin in our lives.

Imagine the consequences if a fireman responded to a fire alarm the way many of us respond to the alarm of guilt. The alarm sounds while the fireman is busily polishing the fire engine. "Oh, no," he says to himself, "there's the fire alarm. That means there's a house burning somewhere. Maybe there are little kids trapped inside. I hate to be reminded of such unpleasant things. I wish there was some way to shut off that awful alarm!" So the fireman stands by the fire engine while the alarm clangs insistently. He wrings his hands and wishes the alarm would leave him alone.

Such a scenario is unthinkable, of course. A fire alarm is a call to action. And so is authentic short-term guilt. It's not a time to wring our hands, stop our ears, or fret and hope the danger will go away. Authentic guilt is a positive, motivating force calling for us to do something in response to sin.

False guilt and burdensome guilt *drive* us to our knees in defeat. But authentic guilt *calls* us to our knees in prayer—a prayer of confession, repentance, and renewal. It is our choice either to respond swiftly to authentic guilt, allowing it to drive us into the arms of a loving God, or to allow it to sour into long-term depression, immobility, and self-hate.

God has provided everything we need to have a complete and fulfilled relationship with Him. Psalm 103:10-12 tells us that God "does not treat us as our sins deserve or repay us according to our iniquities. For as high as the heavens are above the earth, so great is his love for those who fear him; as far as the east is from the west, so far has he removed our transgressions from us." The distance between east and west is absolute infinity—and that's how far God has removed our sins from us. The only thing that causes the onus of sin to cling to us once God has forgiven us is our own will, as we needlessly clutch the guilt of long-dead sins.

Admittedly, releasing our guilt is easier to describe than to do. Few of us are likely to experience sudden, once-and-for all freedom from guilt. Rather, most people find it a step-by-step process of growth toward the full freedom of God's forgiving grace. Let me share with you some of the steps which have enabled me, over the years, to gain liberation from the pain of my past.

The first step is to be honest with yourself. You will never break the grip of guilt so long as you deny the truth about your sins and failures. If you want to be free of guilt you must first accept full responsibility for your sin.

Next, discover God's perspective about your sin. Search out the mind of God by spending time in prayer and by reading his Word. Seek out those passages which deal specifically with sin, repentance, and forgiveness: Psalms 19, 25, 32, 51, and 103; Isaiah 6:1-7; Colossians 1:9-14; 1 John 1:1—2:17. Build the truth of these messages from the heart of God into your own heart.

In the Bible you will discover the basis for a Christian's self-image. You are made in the image of God for the purpose of having fellowship with God. That is the excellence and the glory within you. To lose sight of that excellence, to see yourself only in terms of your sin and failure, is to see yourself falsely. The amazing truth of the Bible is that you are a child of God and he is your loving Father. As you allow this truth to seep into your life, you will sense the fullness of God's forgiveness in your life.

You are stamped with the image of God. But a burden of guilt is like a fun house mirror, distorting your reflection. The self-image you see is not the image of God but a distorted image—an illusion. God, however, sees us through the lens of truth and forgiveness. Through a growing understanding of Scripture, we too can see ourselves through the lens of truth and forgiveness. We can learn to exchange the fun house illusion for the true and exquisite image of a human spirit, once broken by sin, now made whole and pleasing by the grace of a loving God.

The next step for dealing with guilt is to stretch your courage. It takes great courage to live a forgiven life-style. Self-accusing thoughts will pop into your mind just when you feel like you're getting your life under control. People may point the finger of blame at you, wanting you to slink off in shame. It will take courage to stand against internal and external accusations and say, "You have no hold over me. The past is past. I am not without sin, but I am forgiven!"

Finally, become a person who accepts and forgives others. As the healing grace of God seeps deeper and deeper into your life, you will be able to share with others the forgiveness and love you've experienced from God. Your gentle, humble attitude toward others who have fallen will personify Paul's instruction in Galatians 6:1-2: "Brothers, if someone is caught in a sin, you who are spiritual should restore him gently. But watch yourself, or you also may be tempted. Carry each other's burdens, and in this way you will fulfill the law of Christ." Make sure that the grace you have received from God is the grace you give to others.

English playwright Noel Coward was noted for such plays as *Blithe Spirit* and *Private Lives*. But he also was known for his love of mischief and practical jokes. One of Coward's best known pranks involved a demonstration of the power of guilt. He wrote out identical anonymous notes to a dozen of London's most respected men. The note simply read: "Your secret has been discovered. Escape while you can." The morning after the notes were delivered, all 12 men fled the city.

Thanks to the grace of God, you and I don't need to run from guilt. We have complete freedom in the knowledge that our sin has been dissolved and washed away by Jesus Christ. We have exchanged guilt for grace. As we confess our sins, the God of a new beginning is faithful, just, and forgiving. He purifies us from all our guilt and creates for us a clean new heart and a fresh new start.

11

The Truth About Consequences

At 8:45 P.M. on Sunday, August 16, 1987, the control tower at Detroit's Metropolitan Airport cleared Flight 255 for take-off. The cockpit crew had conscientiously completed the pre-flight checklist and determined that all systems for takeoff were "go." But for some unknown reason, the crew neglected to lower the wing flaps and slats which give the plane extra lift during takeoff.

The pilot, a veteran with over twenty thousand hours of flight experience, powered up the engines. The McDonnell Douglas MD-80, carrying a full load of passengers and nearly forty thousand pounds of fuel, began its long, rumbling roar down the runway. The plane finally lifted from the concrete at 215 miles per hour, several hundred feet farther down the runway than was usual for a takeoff. Once airborne, the plane stubbornly refused to climb higher than 50 feet from the ground. Inside the cockpit, a computer-generated voice urgently warned, "Stall! Stall! Stall!" The plane fluttered toward the ground like a falling leaf and slammed into a traffic-laden freeway. The crash took the lives of 160 passengers, crew members, and motorists on the ground.

Only one passenger, a four-year-old girl, survived the disaster.

Humans make mistakes and mistakes have consequences—sometimes tragic consequences. Fundamental laws exist in our world which operate without regard for our wishes. The crew of Flight 255 was powerless to repeal the laws of gravity and aerodynamics which turned a human mistake into a fatal tragedy. Similarly, our personal decisions and actions produce consequences in accordance with fundamental laws of the moral universe. Cause produces effect. Action produces reaction.

I've talked with many people over the years who have suffered intense spiritual agony from the consequences of past choices. I think of Jenny who, in a split-second, made a wrong decision on a California freeway which cost another driver his life. I think of my friend Elliot who made a fateful moral decision one afternoon which abruptly terminated his successful career. I think of Sherry who, as a 17-year-old high school student, made a poor decision regarding the expression of her sexuality. The consequences of her decision included an unwanted pregnancy, an abortion, sterility, depression, and a longing for the lost opportunity for motherhood. I think of a pastor friend of mine who made a tragic moral decision which resulted in scandal and imprisonment.

As calamitous as these cases may be, each of the individuals discovered that, despite their failure, God wasn't finished with them. No matter how they suffered in the aftermath of a sin or mistake, they found a loving heavenly Father who healed them and gave them a new beginning in life. They learned, as you and I are learning, that God is in the business of pouring out blessing and grace, not wrath, on his children.

When we suffer the painful after-effects of sin, it's *not* because God is trying to punish us. All the punishment for our sin has already been received by Jesus Christ upon the cross. The consequences of our sin are simply a part of the impersonal moral order of the universe—the moral equivalent, so to speak, of the law of gravity.

In the created universe, God established both a material and a moral order. When an object falls to the ground, it does so because God's law of gravity is operating in the material order of the universe. You may try to ignore gravity, deny gravity, and even rebel against gravity. But if you take a long walk on a short pier, gravity guarantees you're going to get wet. When you choose to step off the pier and find yourself in water over your head, you can hardly blame God for "punishing" you.

The moral order functions in much the same way. There are consequences associated with the moral choices we make. These consequences are no more God's attempt to punish us or get even with us than getting wet is God's punishment for ignoring gravity by stepping off a pier. On the contrary, God by his grace often shields us from the consequences we deserve for our choices. I'm sure you can recall occasions when you were protected from the full consequences of some sin or mistake. Perhaps there was a time when you nearly caused an accident with your car because of a moment of carelessness or impatience. The accident was miraculously averted and no harm was done—but it easily could have gone the other way. Why didn't it? Because the grace of God was in operation, overruling the consequences of your mistake.

But sometimes there is no way to avoid the consequences of our mistakes. And when the consequences hit us full force, we must deal with them—changing those which are within our power to change. And if there are circumstances we cannot change, we must allow those circumstances to change us. God desires to take the effects of your mistakes and transform them into a beautiful new beginning for your life. The adventure of your new beginning lies in discovering the way God will choose to perform that transformation.

Sometimes it hurts to grow and change. We would rather escape our problems than grow through them. But we must grow—or we will perish. When our dreams die and it becomes clear that our plans must change, we must tap the hidden reservoir of character and courage within us and, with God's help, we must dream new dreams.

"How do I envision a new dream for my life?" you may ask. First, learn to accept the new circumstances in your life with courageous realism. If your reputation has been damaged, it's likely that the damage will not be quickly repaired. If you have hurt someone, you may never win back his or her respect, friendship, or trust. If your career has been destroyed, you must face the fact that it may never be rebuilt. Whatever we are powerless to change must be faced with realism, courage, and faith.

Second, identify the elements of your circumstances which can and should be changed, and appropriate the new beginning God gives you by his grace. God invites you and me to begin again. Why then should we cling to habits of the past which have produced failure in our lives? Take your old patterns of defeatist thinking and self-destructive sin and throw them overboard. You have a new life now. So dedicate your life to a new purpose—serving Christ and others.

Third, learn to identify those things about your calamity that are actually a benefit in your life. Many people come through a period of trial and suffering with a new perspective on life. One businessman I know was toppled by a scandal. After months of depression over his lost power, reputation, and earning ability, he finally recognized that his loss actually reflected God's grace to him. He realized that while he was greedily and ambitiously "gaining the whole world" in his headlong drive to succeed, he was "losing his soul." Today he's thankful for the painful calamity that turned him toward God and gave him a new beginning in life.

Of course, life may not feel like a new beginning to you right now. In fact, it may feel more like "the end." You may be facing an unwanted pregnancy, the death of a marriage or friendship, a crippling lawsuit, bankruptcy, or some other tragedy. You may even be facing the ultimate loss, the loss of your life. I don't intend to offer glib answers or easy solutions. Yet I am convinced that God's grace is close to us even in the worst circumstances of life. We *can* discover God's grace and a new beginning even at the very door of death itself.

My friend Gary made that discovery near the end of his life. Gary was a gifted musician and composer. His charming personality and boyish good looks made him an effective communicator at concerts, evangelistic rallies, and community events.

But Gary was a walking battlefield. Though deeply committed to Jesus Christ, he keenly identified with the words of Paul in Romans 7:15: "I do not understand what I do. For what I want to do I do not do, but what I hate I do." Throughout Gary's life, homosexual tendencies battled his Christian faith for mastery of his life. At times Gary's homosexual tendencies won—and on one of these occasions he was infected with the fatal AIDS virus.

The virus attacked Gary's nervous system. In the end stages of his ordeal, he became blind and lost control of his body functions. He experienced continuous pain. I remember a critical care nurse saying, with eyes full of pity, "This is the worst case of physical suffering I've witnessed in 21 years of nursing." Gary lost 80 pounds over the course of his illness and died at age 32.

I was at his bedside as his emotions see-sawed between hope and depression. I held his hands and prayed with him over his regrets, hurts, and fears. And through all his pain, humiliation, and regret, I saw Gary's faith in God grow.

Fortunately, Gary had a strong sense of being accepted by his loving Father. He didn't view his disease as the judgment of an angry God, but as the natural consequence of some poor moral choices—and, in fact, poor health choices. For the Bible's injunctions against homosexual practice are not just legalistic do's and don'ts. They are amazingly insightful and timely rules for health which make good sense in this or any age.

AIDS is not God's judgment against homosexuals. AIDS is not a vengeance; it's a virus. Today, almost a third of all AIDS victims are heterosexuals, including many who have contracted AIDS as the result of tainted blood transfusions which occurred before present blood screening methods made the blood supply safe. Many AIDS victims are the most innocent victims of all—children. Can we say that AIDS is a plague of judgment upon these people as well? Of course not. AIDS is a predictable consequence of a certain kind of behavior. In his Word, God has given us warnings that are intended to protect us from these consequences by steering us away from the behaviors which provoke them.

In the early months after his diagnosis, Gary began a ministry of witnessing to other AIDS patients in the hospital where he was treated. "Jesus went to the lepers," Gary told me. "He touched them with his grace and they were healed. Well, people with AIDS are the lepers of our day. If Jesus were here today, he'd go to the AIDS ward. But I don't see too many Christians reaching out to people with AIDS. If a pastor comes to the ward, most of these guys just say, 'You don't have any idea what I'm going through.' But they listen to me. Even though I share their disease, they can see the hope in my life. And they want to hear about that hope."

At the onset of his illness, Gary and his wife decided to transform their hurt into healing for others. Since Gary's death, his wife continues the ministry of counseling and helping AIDS victims. Gary's intense pain and suffering is still being transformed into comfort and healing for others through his wife's dedicated service. Many AIDS victims in the last months of their lives are being loved into the kingdom of God.

If you, like my friend Gary, are facing the ultimate loss of imminent death right now, I want you to know that God is very near to you. If you know him in a personal way through his Son Jesus Christ, then he is surrounding you, drawing you to himself. Have you heard those words that Amy Grant sings?

In a little while, we'll be with the Father.
Can't you see him smile?
In a little while, we'll be home forever,
In awhile....[1]

None of us knows how many years God, in his grace, will
give him upon this earth. Many people I've known, who have
received a grim medical prognosis, have outlived their doctors' predictions by years. And sadly, many young people who
might have expected a life of 70 years or more have been cut
down by accident or disease in their childhood, teens, or
twenties. But even though we do not all receive the standard
allotment of "three score years and ten" in this life, we all
receive 24 hours each day. No matter how many hours remain for you in this life, you can still choose to seize each one
and live it to the honor of God.

One way you can transform your life into a hymn of praise
to God is by becoming a healer—a *wounded* healer. Look
around you. There are other people close to you. They are
dying without hope, without any sense that they will be
received by the loving Father you serve. Who can better
understand their pain and fear than you? Who can be a more
compassionate listener? Who can be a better friend to them
than you?

But what if you don't have this hope to share? Perhaps the
loving Father I described in these pages is a stranger to you.
You have never made a commitment of your life to Jesus
Christ. What then? I want you to know that the God of a new
beginning is very near to you. He pleads with you to begin
again. He offers you a newness of life beyond any life you
could imagine on this earth—a life in eternity with him.

It doesn't matter what kind of life you have lived. It doesn't
matter how many days of life you have left. Luke 23:39-46
records the last few moments of Jesus' life. As he was being
crucified along with two criminals, one of them turned to
Jesus and said, "Jesus, remember me when you come into

your kingdom." And Jesus replied, "I tell you the truth, today you will be with me in paradise."

This crucified criminal was a man whose total Christian life was measured not in years but minutes—and they were minutes filled with incredible agony. But the grace of the God of a new beginning touched him and transformed him. His earthly life as a believer was brief, but his life began again—in eternity.

I pray that this man's hope of a new beginning in heaven is your hope as well. A new life with Christ in eternity is the most profound kind of new beginning imaginable. And it is a life that has no end.

12

Dream a New Dream

The little ship hurtled up the side of a monstrous wave, wallowed momentarily on its crest, then careened helplessly down into a deep trough. Angry waves rose above the small craft like towering foam-capped mountains threatening to collapse and bury it under tons of water.

The terrified crew clung to the rigging and cried to their gods for mercy. They had tossed every scrap of cargo overboard to lighten the ship. Yet the waves continued to wash over its sides, filling the holds and swamping the vessel.

The captain staggered down into the rolling hold. Amazed, he saw a man asleep on a wooden bunk, just out of reach of the water that sloshed about the hold. "Jonah!" he cried, shaking the man. "How can you sleep? The ship is about to break apart! Get up and call on your God!"

Roused from his deep sleep, Jonah rose wearily and followed the captain up to the deck. The seamen were rolling dice made of bone, casting lots to determine which crewman had angered his god, bringing calamity upon them all. Jonah was not surprised when the lot fell upon him. All eyes transfixed Jonah with suspicion and fear.

"Where do you come from?" they demanded. "Who are your people? And who is your God?"

"I am a Hebrew," answered Jonah. "I worship Jehovah, the God of heaven, who made the sea and the land." Jonah's words terrified the sailors. They knew he was fleeing from his God, for he had already told them so. But they had no idea that his God was so powerful, the Creator of all that is.

"What should we do to you to make the sea calm down for us?" they asked.

"Throw me into the sea," Jonah replied. But the men were afraid to do so, fearing that by murdering this man they would be subject to even worse punishment.

They attempted to row the ship to shore, but the storm's intensity increased. At last, with a terrified prayer for mercy to Jonah's incomprehensibly powerful God, they threw Jonah into the sea. Jonah disappeared beneath the convulsing waves. Within moments the raging storm abated and the ship rocked gently on the suddenly tranquil surface of the Mediterranean. The grateful sailors pledged themselves by vows and sacrifice to the God of their lost comrade Jonah.

Swallowed! That's a descriptive title for Jonah's ordeal as described in Jonah 1:1-17. Jonah descended into the deep where he was swallowed by the sea, swallowed by a great fish, and swallowed by horror and fear. For three days and nights Jonah was buried in the misery, stench, and darkness of the fish's belly. He had time to contemplate and regret. Why was he in such extreme circumstances? Where had he gone wrong? What would God do with him now? Jonah knew he had no one to blame but himself.

Once he walked with God as a servant, doing God's will and seeking God's direction for his life. But somewhere he strayed and neglected his relationship with God. So Jonah was a soul-weary, spiritually depleted man on the day God came to him with a special mission: "Go to the great city of Nineveh and preach against it, because its wickedness has come up before me."

In his depleted state, Jonah refused God's leading for his life. He fled from God, seeking a place where he could be his own boss, set his own agenda, and assert his own will. He exchanged relationship with God for rebellion against God. And it was this fateful choice which ultimately dragged Jonah down into the cold depths of the Mediterranean where he languished, drenched in the digestive juices of a sea monster.

Finally Jonah's rebellious spirit was broken by the misery of his self-made hell. He prayed to the God of a new beginning for deliverance:

> You hurled me into the deep, into the very heart of the seas, and the currents swirled about me; all your waves and breakers swept over me.... The engulfing waters threatened me, the deep surrounded me; seaweed was wrapped around my head....
>
> When my life was ebbing away, I remembered you, LORD, and my prayer rose to you, to your holy temple.
>
> Those who cling to worthless idols forfeit the grace that could be theirs. But I, with a song of thanksgiving, will sacrifice to you. What I have vowed I will make good. Salvation comes from the LORD (Jonah 2:3,5,7-8).

And the God of grace gave Jonah a new beginning. He delivered him from the fish and from the sea, and he cast Jonah up onto a sandy beach. Though he had been buried three days in a watery grave, he now experienced resurrection and a new opportunity to fulfil God's plan for his life.

As Jonah lay exhausted and hungry on the beach, the Lord spoke to him again: "Go to the great city of Nineveh and proclaim to it the message I give you" (Jonah 3:2). In obedient response, Jonah rose weakly to his feet, brushed the sand from his body, and turned his face toward Nineveh.

And he began to walk.

When Pastor Buckingham read the story of Jonah, he felt he was reading his own biography. Like Jonah, he was a full-time servant of God who rebelled. Jonah fled from God physically, boarding a ship headed away from Ninevah and God's will. But Pastor Buckingham fled God secretly, covering his secret sins with a veneer of pastoral piety.

As a pastor in South Carolina, Buckingham was confronted by his church board with evidence of an adulterous affair. He could not bluff his way out of it. He could not hide it. He could not excuse it. His sin was exposed and he was terrified.

After the board meeting, which ended in the pastor's dismissal, Buckingham's wife found him in the dark church basement, huddled in a fetal position, crying uncontrollably. "It would be better for you, for the children, and for this church if I were dead," he wept.

Defeated and jobless, Pastor Buckingham returned with his family to his home state of Florida. He manipulated his way into a new pastorate, convincing the church leadership to hire him without checking his past. The first few months in his new church were like a honeymoon. But soon the rumors of adultery, lies, and manipulative power plays filtered down to Florida from South Carolina. Buckingham's adultery was all in the past, but his deceit and manipulation had continued in his new setting. "The Holy Spirit," he later confessed, "was not controlling my life."

Rocked by rumors of their pastor's hidden sins, the Florida church cast Buckingham into the troubled sea just as the pagan sailors had sacrificed Jonah to the turmoil he had caused. One Sunday morning Pastor Buckingham stepped to the pulpit to begin his sermon. Lying on the pulpit was a petition, with over three hundred signatures, demanding his resignation. Shocked and stunned, he somehow managed to deliver his sermon and complete the service.

After the service, the pastor learned that a 47-page detective agency report on his background, commissioned by one of the elders, had been distributed to the church members. The report was filled with shameful truths mingled with terrible half-truths, inaccuracies, and lies.

Pastor Buckingham's ministry in the Florida church was destroyed. His usefulness to God and his Church seemed to be at an end. Before him stretched an endless expanse of anxiety, regret, and the dark unknown of the future. Like Jonah, Pastor Buckingham had been swallowed up by failure, disgrace, and remorse. His ministry had reached a pitiful dead end.

Pastor Buckingham's story might easily have ended there—except for the grace of the God of a new beginning. Since all his time was "spare time," the deposed pastor did a lot of reading. As he thumbed through a copy of *Guideposts* magazine, he noticed an announcement of a writing contest. Challenged by the contest, he submitted a written profile of a missionary friend of his. Out of two thousand submissions, his story was one of the 20 winners. His accomplishment led to an assignment for a major Christian book publisher. Though stripped of his old dreams, ex-Pastor Buckingham was suddenly given a *new* dream—the dream of ministering to people as a Christian writer.

Today, Jamie Buckingham is the author of dozens of Christian books including *A Way Through The Wilderness, Risky Living,* and *Where Eagles Soar,* describing his fall and his rebirth as an authentic man of God. Having dealt firmly with the sinful patterns of his past, Jamie Buckingham now dreams a new dream and lives a new life, of which he writes:

> Perfection still eludes me. I am still vulnerable. But most important, I am no longer satisfied with my imperfection. Nor, thank God, am I intimidated by it. I have reached the point of recognizing that God uses imperfect, immoral, dishonest people. In fact, that's all there are these days. All the holy men seem to have gone off and died. There's no one left but us sinners to carry on the ministry.[1]

Jamie Buckingham is right: there are no perfect people in this world. But God is in the process of doing a perfect work through fallible, failure-prone people like you and me. God can use our pain and failure to bring good to our lives and praise to himself. God's work in us is a process of transformation and change. It is frequently a painful process, a journey that leads us through valleys of despair, depression, and desperation.

When our old dreams die, we feel a paralyzing sense of confusion in life. When we lose direction we become disoriented. When we depart the clearly marked path of God's will we find ourselves in a swamp, sinking and feeling totally alone. Of this feeling, J.I. Packer writes:

> If I found I had driven into a bog, I should know I had missed the road. But this knowledge would not be of much comfort if I then had to stand helpless watching the car sink and vanish: the damage would be done, and that would be that. Is it the same when a Christian wakes up to the fact that he has missed God's guidance and taken the wrong way? Is the damage irrevocable? Must he now be put off course for life? Thank God, no. Our God is a God who not merely restores, but takes up our mistakes and follies into his plan for us and brings good out of them. This is part of the wonder of his gracious sovereignty. "I will restore to you the years that the locust hath eaten...and ye shall eat in plenty, and be satisfied, and praise the name of the LORD your God, that hath dealt wondrously with you" [Joel 2:25-26, KJV].[2]

God is the God of a new beginning. He delights in creating something out of nothing, in bringing good out of evil, and in transforming abysmal failure into stratospheric success. Genesis 1 records that God created matter out of total void. Then from chaotic, formless matter he brought about the order and beauty of the heavens and earth. God looked upon all he made and called it good.

The God of the first genesis is also the God of a *new* genesis—the new beginning. He takes pleasure in refashioning the chaos and emptiness of our lives into something orderly and splendid. And when we have come through that transformation process, he looks upon our lives with favor and satisfaction and calls it good. As Paul tells us in Romans 8:28-29 (NASB), "And we know that God causes all things to work together for good to those who love God, to those who are called according to His purpose. For whom He foreknew, He also predestined to become conformed to the image of His Son, that He might be the first-born among many brethren." Everything that happens to us—joy or sorrow, success or failure—is focused in the mind of God on one goal: making us more like Jesus Christ.

God is at work for his good in our lives. This doesn't mean that everything that happens to us in life *feels* good. As M. Scott Peck says in *The Road Less Traveled*:

> Life is difficult. This is a great truth, one of the greatest truths. It is a great truth because once we truly see this truth, we transcend it. Once we truly know that life is difficult—once we truly understand and accept it—then life is no longer difficult. Because once it is accepted, the fact that life is difficult no longer matters.[3]

Life is seldom more difficult than when our old dream dies and the new dream is not yet in view. At that moment we can only see the loss; we can't yet glimpse the opportunity. Our inclination is to seek the security of the familiar. The thought of relinquishing our cherished dreams and following God in a totally new direction frightens us. We prefer the comfort of the known—even clinging to known sins, known pain, and known patterns of failure—to the risky adventure of faith in God. We would rather cling to our disease than be made whole by the unerring scalpel of the Great Physician.

Becoming people of a new beginning—people who dare to dream a new dream—means becoming people of courage. Our courage to face the future is rooted in a realistic reliance upon God who emboldens our hearts with these words from Isaiah 43:18-19: "Forget the former things; do not dwell on the past. See, I am doing a new thing! Now it springs up; do you not perceive it? I am making a way in the desert and streams in the wasteland."

Chuck Colson had to learn to forget the former things and find God's way through the desert. In his tragic fall from power during the Watergate scandal, Colson lost his reputation, his prestigious position as special counsel to President Nixon, his income, and his freedom. After he emerged from more than a year in prison, Colson had some decisions to make. Would he accept responsibility for his wrong choices or shift the blame to the hostile press, disloyal White House colleagues, or the fickle public? Would he allow God to chart a new course for his life or cling to the dead, barren past?

Colson decided to face the uncertainty of the future with courage, a desire to serve others, and a goal of transforming his failures into a ministry of healing. Since making that choice, Colson has challenged thousands of people through his books, personal appearances, and media interviews to discover a brand-new life in Christ. He is passionately involved in the movement to reform our country's dehumanizing and ineffectual prison system. His life bears eloquent witness of God's power to transform human brokenness into healing for others.

I think the story of Joseph, contained in the last 15 chapters of Genesis, is one of the most appealing and fascinating stories in the Bible. It's the story of a righteous man who suffered continual betrayal and mistreatment at the hands of family, friends, and employers. Joseph was sold into slavery by his jealous and hateful brothers. As the servant of an Egyptian officer, Joseph was imprisoned on a false charge of attempted rape after his master's wife tried unsuccessfully to seduce him. In prison, Joseph befriended the king's former butler. But after the butler's release he betrayed his promise to help Joseph. For two more years Joseph languished in prison.

For many years, Joseph suffered terrible and unjust abuses. Then God exalted him to a position of enormous power and influence in Egypt, second only to that of Pharaoh. Joseph had many painful memories and resentful feelings to resolve. He enjoyed a position of such unquestioned authority that he could have easily exacted revenge against everyone who had hurt him—his brothers, his previous master's wife, and the butler. But instead he chose to live by grace. He became a man of a new beginning.

When Joseph's first two sons were born, he gave them names which reflected the condition of his heart. He named his firstborn Manasseh, a word which means "God has taken the sting out of my memories." He named his second son Ephraim, meaning "twice fruitful," because God had made him fruitful in the land of his suffering. Joseph named his sons in a profound gesture of gratitude to God for the two-fold new beginning God had given him. First, God healed Joseph's memories and enabled him to move forward in his life without bitterness or regret. Second, God rewarded Joseph with extraordinary fruitfulness and success against a backdrop of suffering, slavery, and injustice.

How was God able to take the sting out of Joseph's memories? I believe that Joseph's memories were healed largely because Joseph made an attitude choice. Long before Manasseh was born, I believe Joseph gave birth to a *spiritual* Manasseh in his heart. Joseph consciously decided to relinquish his bitterness, hatred, and self-pity. He deliberately chose to banish all self-consuming, self-destructive passions from his life. Joseph seemed to understand that the only power the past has over our emotions is the power we allow it to have. We can clutch the smoldering coal of bitterness to our hearts until it eventually kills us. Or we can release the bitterness of the past and cling instead to the grace of God, trusting him to create a new beginning for our lives.

In his book, *The Light Within You,* John Claypool tells of a man who desperately needed a new beginning and a Manasseh-like healing for his memories. The man was drinking and got into a bitter argument with his wife. In his rage, the man ran out of his house, started his car, and backed recklessly down the driveway. He didn't know that his three-year-old son had followed him out of the house and was behind the car as he angrily backed toward the street. The man jammed on the brakes in horror as he looked across the hood at the crushed and lifeless little body of his son lying on the concrete driveway.

Yet the God of a new beginning was at work even in this awful tragedy. The little boy was dead and the gruesome event was burned indelibly into the father's memory. But through the care and counseling of Claypool and other Christians, the man was able to experience the forgiveness of God. He also experienced *Manasseh,* the healing of his memories. The terrible memory of his son's death will never disappear. But the sting of the memory has gradually receded as God's grace has slowly seeped into his mind and heart.

This man also learned that he could turn his pain into ministry to others. He began to dream a new dream. He gave himself in service to others, becoming an organizer of one of the most effective Scouting movements in the southeastern United States. He was not trying to earn forgiveness. Rather, he was gratefully responding to God's forgiveness by doing for thousands of other boys what he could no longer do for his own son.

As we have seen in the story of the prodigal son and the loving father, the key to receiving and responding to God's forgiveness is knowing who God is. We must understand that God is a loving, forgiving Father. His heart is full of mercy and he is ready to give us a new beginning in life. "The only answer to the sin problem," John Claypool concludes, "is the

Father, and the only way to deal with our guilt is to go to him as the prodigal turned toward home and gave himself over to mercy and to restitution and to reformation."[4]

Like the prodigal, we have a loving Father. And our Father is ready and waiting to change our worst hurts into triumphs of his amazing grace. Because the God of a new beginning is our Father, we are children of the Infinite. When the old dreams die, he is alongside us, helping us to dream a new dream. And dreams that come from the heart of God really do come true.

13

Alone Again

Tick, tick, tick, tick . . .
It was the sound of time passing, measured second by lonely second in the steady rhythms of the hall clock. A man sat at the dining room table, a pen poised over the blank pages of his journal. Slowly he lowered the penpoint to the page and began to write:

> It's been two weeks since Karen walked out on me, taking the children with her. I don't know where my family is. The papers arrived from her attorney this morning. I can't believe this is really happening to me, to us.
>
> Dear God, I don't want this divorce to happen. I know you're here in my darkness, but I can't see you. I know you love me, but that love seems empty and unreal right now.
>
> I used to take this home for granted when it was full of laughter and life. Now it's just a house. Every room is full of emptiness. The bed is cold. My heart

keeps on beating because it doesn't have the sense
to know that my life is over.

Tick, tick, tick, tick . . .

He closed the notebook and set the pen down on the table.
He leaned back in his chair and sighed. He looked out the
window and wondered what he was doing there in the gath-
ering dusk, silent and alone with his depression. Then it
occurred to him: he was waiting. And he had no idea what he
was waiting for.

That's what it's like to be alone again, whether through
death or divorce. Silence. Loneliness. Grief. Regret. Waiting.
Waiting for the pain to end and for a new chapter to begin.

If you've been through a divorce or the death of your spouse,
you know all about it—all the feelings, all the pain, all the
anxiety. But what you may not be aware of is that there can
be life and love and a new beginning somewhere beyond the
valley of your loss. The exact form of your new beginning
cannot even be glimpsed while you are in the immediate
aftermath of your loss. That is where the waiting comes in.
We don't like to wait, yet if we are honest before God and his
Word, we know that waiting is a crucial ingredient in God's
process of maturing us and molding us to become more like
his Son, Jesus Christ. "Be still before the LORD," says Psalm
37:7, "and wait patiently for him."

Tick, tick, tick, tick . . .

Time passes. The pain lingers. We plead with the Lord for
a glimpse of a new beginning beyond grief, beyond loss,
beyond regret, beyond guilt. In Ecclesiastes 3:1 and 11, God
replies, "There is a time for everything, and a season for
every activity under heaven. . . . He has made everything
beautiful in its time."

Questions haunt the mind: How will I cope with all the
details my spouse used to take care of? Can I survive finan-
cially? Should I remarry? Will anyone ever want me again?
These questions cannot be answered all at once. We must
have time to recover, time to heal. And whether we like it or

not, people who have been through the loss of their mate need a minimum of two, three, or more years to allow the emotional, spiritual, and legal dust to settle before a new beginning starts to emerge.

But there's good news: The first few years after the end of a marriage don't have to be wasted years. Approached with determination and a hopeful attitude, the aftermath of a divorce or a death of a spouse—though a time of sorrow and suffering—can also be a time of growth, renewal, and learning. As A.W. Tozer has said, "We should be watchful lest we lose any blessing which suffering might bring." When we choose to be teachable and flexible, God can open some amazing possibilities to us. Let's look at some of these possibilities.

Consider the possibility of deeper devotion to God. I have always found it perplexing that single people—whether unmarried, divorced, or widowed—are so often assigned a second-place status in the church. I find in the Scriptures that single and single-again people seem to have a unique and honorable place in the body of Christ. This doesn't mean I am downgrading marriage—far from it! Rather I believe it's time we upgrade the place single, divorced, and widowed people are generally given in the church. As Paul wrote in 1 Corinthians 7:32-35,

> I would like you to be free from concern: An unmarried man is concerned about the Lord's affairs—how he can please the Lord. But a married man is concerned about the affairs of this world—how he can please his wife—and his interests are divided. An unmarried woman or virgin is concerned about the Lord's affairs: Her aim is to be devoted to the Lord in both body and spirit. But a married woman is concerned about the affairs of this world—how she can please her husband. I am saying this for your own good, not to restrict you, but that you may

live in a right way in undivided devotion to the Lord.

Paul goes on to make clear that it is no sin to be married. It is right and good that a married person be attentive to the needs of his or her mate. But it is also inevitable that a married person will have less time to devote to single-minded Christian service.

Marriage is a beautiful gift, ordained by God. Married people have a scriptural duty to invest quality time in their families. That's a central part of their ministry as Christians. But the unmarried person has his or her own special place in the body of Christ. We should not fix on remarriage as the only kind of new beginning God can give us after a divorce or the death of a spouse. In fact, God's gift of a new beginning for your life could be the gift of singleness.

Divorce is an incredibly painful experience. For most people, divorce is equally as painful as the loss of a loved one. When we find ourselves alone again, we need to draw close to God and cling to him for dear life. This is a time when you discover that God really is your all-sufficient Friend. Having lost close loved ones myself, I've known the deep depression and loneliness that accompanies grief. And I can assure you that God *is* there through your time of trial. He *is* sufficient.

Another possibility God reveals in our lives following a loss or divorce is *greater openness*. Part of the growth God wants to bring about in us is an eagerness for change, for new experiences, for new relationships. A major disruption in our lives such as divorce or loss brings pain. But it also brings an opportunity for us to deepen our friendship with God and with others, to discover new goals in life, and to develop new coping skills. We learn life by living; we build confidence by risking. Bit by bit, moment by moment, we learn that we can take risks in life and in relationships, that we can become vulnerable in sharing ourselves with others, and that having risked we are still accepted.

Still another possibility God reveals to us at the end of a marriage is a *stronger individual identity*. During your marriage you were defined, at least to some degree, by your relationship to your mate. Now you are alone again—and you have an opportunity to learn anew who you really are. You have an opportunity to develop new interests, to meet new challenges, to explore new opportunities in your career or your ministry for God. As you aggressively seek to grow, you will discover that this growth process is the key to the joy, satisfaction and healthy self-image you seek in life.

Divorce is hard on your self-image. In the maelstrom of conflict, accusation, and hostility that usually surrounds a marital breakup, the inner you is mercilessly buffeted by withering emotional forces. But God wants to encourage you to discover his healing for your broken self-image. As John Claypool has said, "To accept yourself positively and live creatively is the way to joy, but to deny and reject God's gift of yourself is the way to ruin." So when you arise each new morning, say a prayer of thanks to God for the gift of who you are. Focus on the joy of knowing God, of being a child of your loving Father. As God progressively discloses deeper and richer insights into your gifts and qualities as a special human being, you'll find you don't need to be married to be a complete person—and you'll find you really like the special person you are.

Finally, God wants to reveal to you a deeper experience of *personal independence*. Many people marry out of need and insecurity—and into a state of dependency. If you are a dependent, insecure person, then you know that even if you have suffered great pain in your marriage relationship, you've relied upon your spouse to meet your needs, to calm your fears, to supply the things you lacked in yourself. You have been dependent. It has been said that in a divorce, you always get custody of yourself. Whether your loss is due to divorce or death, you now have self-custody, you are now self-dependent. This fact may frighten you, but it can also challenge and exhilarate you and enable you to grow!

Christian counselor Jim Smoke notes that, in case after case he has observed, people grow to meet the challenges of life after marriage. In *Living Beyond Divorce*, he writes,

> A man living beyond divorce chooses to live on frozen dinners, eat out, starve, or learn to cook. I am amazed at how many have chosen the latter. Self-responsibility says, "I will do what I need to do to live." This doesn't mean that you simply go in pursuit of someone to do your cooking for you. It means that you learn the process and grow because of it. . . .
>
> Many women have expressed a hopelessness in taking care of house and auto after a divorce. If it was always done by the man of the house, then you will simply have to learn. Classes are offered at colleges in both these categories. Those who have learned have a strong feeling of pride in their accomplishment.[1]

There is life after divorce or the loss of your spouse—and that life can be an adventure. You are learning that you can live the adventure without being rescued by a spouse. And most important, you are learning in a deeper way what it means to *rely upon God*.

Dependent people tend to remarry too soon because they are desperate for someone to lean on. Remarriage is a possibility for you, but it is not a necessity. If you start to develop a promising relationship with a marriageable person, take great care. Go slowly and give your relationship time to develop. Make sure that you are being motivated toward remarriage by God's leading and by authentic love, not by panic or insecurity. Share your heart very honestly with the other person, and make sure he or she is being open with you. Be a good listener. Set the pattern for meaningful communication now, and avoid tragic surprises later.

At the same time, keep in close touch with your friends, your support group. Be accountable to them and seek their counsel about the relationship you are building. If someone shares misgivings about this other person in your life, don't be defensive or too quick to dismiss their concerns. Make sure that you want to marry that person to contribute to his or her happiness and well-being, not just to fulfill your own needs and happiness. Most of all, learn to seek security in God rather than another person. People can let you down; God will never let you down. True security is found in him alone.

Loneliness, panic, anxiety, fear, insecurity, depression—these are your enemies in the depths of your loss or divorce. At this crucial time, you may be prone to making poor decisions, motivated by negative impulses rather than by reason and wisdom. So set aside time to pray, to reflect, and to analyze your life. Don't just "kill time" or fill times of loneliness with self-pity. Instead, fill your life with things that build your inner self: good books, meditation and prayer, and supportive friends.

The pain of a loved one's death cuts deep, and there is a sense in which this hurt never completely heals. Nor would we want it to. There is a poignancy, a bittersweet tinge in our memories of a lost loved one. For the hurt to completely heal, the memory would have to die. Yet it is good to savor those memories and keep them alive.

The pain of divorce is similar to that of grief, yet it has its own special sting and poignancy. As Jim Smoke points out, "The difference between the death of a mate and the divorce of a mate is that death leaves you with a file of good memories of yesterday while divorce leaves you with a 'ring-around-the-collar' memory of yesterday. Any good memories prior to divorce tend to be long forgotten after the divorce."[2]

When we have been wounded by grief or divorce we need to be healed in our memories. This does not mean we desire amnesia, the obliteration of our mental record of the past. Rather, we seek to remove the sting from those memories. In some ways, a painful memory is similar to a physical wound.

With proper treatment, a physical wound heals, leaving a scar that may be unsightly, but is approximately as healthy as the surrounding tissue. In the same way, a properly treated emotional wound can also be healed. The scar of the memory remains, and it's not pretty to look at. But the sting and the trauma can't hurt us anymore.

An untreated physical wound can become infected, gangrenous, and even fatal. But an untreated emotional wound simply continues to ooze and sting. Eventually such emotional infections can rob us of joy, love, and life itself. What is an untreated emotional wound? It is a painful memory which we have allowed to be infected with such poisons as wounded pride, self-pity, lust for revenge, unresolved anger, bitterness, malice, slander, and an irreconcilable spirit. These are corrosive emotional impulses. Unless they are overcome in your life, they will continue to hurt you. They may even destroy you.

In the process of a divorce, we find ourselves subject to enormously unfair forces. We are pierced by outrageous accusations. We are subjected to hostility and contempt. We may even suffer mistreatment, misunderstanding, or pressure from friends or family. Through all of this, there will be a tendency for us to want to strike back, to avenge ourselves, to feel sorry for ourselves. But we will never experience healing in our memories until we begin to live by the advice of Paul in Romans 12:17,19, and 21: Do not repay anyone evil for evil. . . . Do not take revenge, my friends, but leave room for God's wrath, for it is written: 'It is mine to avenge; I will repay,' says the Lord. . . . Do not be overcome by evil, but overcome evil with good."

Decide not to speak critically about your ex-spouse, especially before your children. You are making an important impression on the lives of your children at this crucial time in your life. They are watching to see how you react in the tough times of life. Are you going to set an example of bitterness or Christlike grace? Whatever you do, don't allow your children to become victims of your divorce.

And what if your ex-spouse unfairly criticizes you to your children? Don't retaliate. Children can see which parent is responding with grace and maturity. If necessary, explain to your children that your ex-spouse has some problems of perception and needs their prayers and understanding for that spirit of bitterness. Try to stir up good memories and positive feelings in your children. As you help your children to unconditionally love your ex-mate, you will be surprised to see how your own capacity for unconditional love begins to grow.

A few years ago, I saw the healing process begin in one woman's life somewhere in the skies over the Atlantic Ocean. This woman was a stewardess on a flight taking a number of pastors and laymen to observe and assist the work of World Vision to alleviate physical and spiritual hunger in western Africa.

During our 14-hour flight, I sat next to my friend Al vom Steeg, the pastor of St. Luke's Methodist Church in Fresno, California. We were talking together about emotional and spiritual healing, and a flight attendant, Cindy, overheard our conversation. She introduced herself and said she had been divorced for almost two years.

"I just can't let go of all the awful things Cliff did to me," she said. "He lied to me constantly, abused me psychologically, manipulated me, and continually tried to tear down my self-image. He was sleeping with another woman for about a year before I found out about it."

She paused a moment to pull out a handkerchief and dab at her eyes. "Even after I found out about the affair," she continued, "I still loved him and wanted to hold our marriage together. I tried to get him to go to counseling with me. But he decided he'd rather leave me and live with this other woman. Whenever I think of Cliff I just hate him! I hate every memory of him! I know it's not right to feel this way, but I don't know how to help it."

"These feelings are probably manifesting themselves as physical problems, aren't they?" I asked, recalling my own attempts to repress grief or anger, resulting in insomnia and digestive disorders.

Cindy nodded. "I've had a lot of trouble sleeping. A lot of stomach troubles too."

"It seems to me," said Al, "that you've become immobilized by your resentment and bitterness toward this man."

"Immobilized," Cindy repeated. "That's exactly how I feel."

As the three of us continued to share and pray together, Al said something I'll never forget—something I don't think Cindy will ever forget either. "Cindy, until you allow yourself to forgive Cliff, you are allowing him to control you. You ought not let anyone control you except God."

This insight made a profound impact on Cindy. "That's right," she said. "I'm letting Cliff control me! Well, he's not going to control me anymore. From now on I'm under God's control."

I'm sure Cindy had a lot of healing ahead of her, a lot of letting go to do. But a miracle began in her heart that day. There in the skies over the Atlantic, this young woman experienced the beginning of a new beginning.

So it is with you and me. The healing of painful memories takes place in our hearts as we learn, day by day, instant by instant, to be controlled not by anger and self-pity, but by the forgiveness and unconditional love of God.

If you have lost a partner to death rather than divorce, the pain of your memories is probably of a quite different kind. It is not bitterness and anger you wrestle with, but longing and loss. Sometime after my friend Leighton Ford suffered the death of his son Sandy, he shared with me that he supposed that time does indeed heal the hurt a bit, but times does not heal completely. As time passes, the hurt recedes somewhat, but you also experience a lot of "ambushes." I wasn't sure at the time what he meant about being "ambushed" by memories, but since the death of my brother Paul, I know exactly what he meant.

I experienced such an ambush not long ago when a popular song from the early '60s came on the radio, a song called "Donna." The song packed a powerful nostalgic punch because of the memories it stirred up. Paul and I were teenagers when that song was popular. My brother had a girlfriend named Donna at the time. He bought a 45 RPM record of that song and we played it often on Paul's phonograph.

I was shaving at the sink in the bathroom when that song came on the radio and ambushed me with 25-year-old memories tinged with sadness. That's the way grief is. We can be going about our normal lives when suddenly a song or a memento or a thought will come to us. We are suddenly ambushed by grief.

Whatever your hurts, whatever your memories, the best place to find God's healing grace and a new beginning is within a supportive community of close Christian friends. We need the fellowship of people who are growing, adventurous, and positive in their outlook. Those few special friends who accept and affirm you through your crisis are your family, your counselors, your life-support system. Nurture these relationships and seek the wise counsel of discerning friends who demonstrate a strong, practical understanding of Scripture. Learn to lean on your friends and let them into your life in a new and deeper way.

If you are divorced, you don't need anyone to tell you that divorce isn't God's best plan for your life. You know that divorce solves few problems; and it creates enormous new problems. You know about all the financial and legal entanglements, the tensions in mingled families, the emotional trauma, the guilt, and the regret. But you also know that divorce sometimes happens even after we have done our best to reconcile. Divorce is sometimes even imposed upon us against our will by a destructive, adulterous, or irreconcilable mate.

Some well-meaning people may have lectured you or quoted Scripture at you. Some less well-meaning people may have even judged you or turned their backs on you. But I want you to know that there is one who always accepts you right where you are, and he wants nothing more than to give you a new beginning in life. He is your loving Father, God himself. In Malachi 2:16, God says, "I hate divorce." The reason God hates divorce is that he hates the pain, misery, and destruction of relationships that divorce brings. Yes, God hates divorce. But he loves divorced people. Unfortunately, there are many churches that assign a second-class status to divorced Christians. But there are also many churches that vibrantly demonstrate God's love for all people, regardless of marital status. If you are made to feel second-class in your present church, you may want to seek a church home where you will be accepted as the first-class person you really are.

People who have come to the end of a marriage are people to be handled with care—a great deal of loving care. If you are a friend to such a person right now, I encourage you to become that person's *best* friend. There are a lot of people who will reach out to others in the moment of a sudden loss. But there are very few who will stand by grieving people over the long haul, over the months and years they will need to find true healing and a new beginning.

Alone again people need practical help. This is especially true of single parents who are struggling to hold a family together, maintain a job, and keep themselves together emotionally at the same time. Offer to take care of the children and give that single parent the night off. Help with the household chores. Fix the broken fence. Take the car in for servicing. Mow the lawn. Clean the leaves out of the rain gutters. Help paint the house. Single parents have needs, and they probably won't call out for help. You have to see the need and offer to meet it.

Shelly and Nina are back-fence neighbors in a northern California suburb. They're both in their 30s, both members of the same church. Shelly is a recently-divorced single parent working days as a retail clerk. Nina is a full time homemaker who has experienced marital problems for several years. Once a week, on Shelly's day off, Shelly puts on a pot of coffee and Nina brings over some donuts and they have a coffee break and pray together.

One day, Nina came over to find Shelly in a depressed mood. Shelly began complaining about her life as a divorcee. She felt rejected, bitter, and angry. She was having a lot of trouble with her children. She wasn't happy with the day-care center she was using. Bills and bounced checks were mounting because her ex-husband was increasingly late with his child-support payments. Nina listened to Shelly's complaints in silence for a few minutes. Then she exploded.

"At least your husband is out of the house!" Nina shouted as Shelly's eyes widened. "I wish I was divorced like you! All Jack and I ever do is scream at each other! My stomach is in knots all the time! I've even started smoking again! On top of that, you want me to sit here and listen while you whine and complain about how hard your life is! You know something, Shelly? I envy you for being divorced!"

For a few long moments Shelly and Nina glared at each other with eyes full of anger and hurt. Then Shelly reached across the table and took Nina's hands in hers. "We're such fools!" said Shelly, laughing through the tears that filled her eyes.

"Oh Shelly, I'm so sorry," said Nina, taking a paper napkin and wiping Shelly's tears first, then her own. "I guess we each have our own pain, don't we? Yours is just as real as mine. I wouldn't trade places with you for anything in the world."

We each have our own pain. We are waiting in our new-found state of alone-ness—waiting to see what kind of new beginning God is going to bring about in our lives. "Be still before the LORD," says Psalm 37:7, "and wait patiently for him." So, obediently, we wait.

Tick, tick, tick, tick . . .

By God's grace, we are learning not to wait passively, but creatively. We are using our time of solitude to learn, to stretch, to grow. One day we will look back and we will be able to say, as in the words of Psalm 40:1-3, "I waited patiently for the Lord; he turned to me and heard my cry. He lifted me out of the slimy pit, out of the mud and mire; he set my feet on a rock and gave me a firm place to stand. He put a new song in my mouth, a hymn of praise to our God."

14

The Deep Places of the Soul

It happened on an unusually warm and clear San Francisco day in July 1987. Lanie drove her late-model Buick along Doyle Drive under a canopy of golden sun and blue sky. The bright green lawns and stately groves of the Presidio lined her route and the warm breeze flowed through the open windows.

The drive took 35-year-old Lanie to the Golden Gate Bridge. She drove across the bridge and pulled off the road when she reached the Sausalito side. She got out of her car and walked back onto the bridge to a place known as the Eleventh Pole, where the span reaches its highest elevation. She stood poised at the edge of the bridge for a couple seconds, then stepped off the bridge and into eternity.

Anyone's death is a tragedy, but there is something especially heartbreaking about suicide. Life is a struggle for dignity, love, and meaning. There is a nobility in the struggle for life. I'm not talking about merely gasping for one more breath or straining to survive physically. Rather, I'm talking about the struggle to truly, authentically *live*. It is ennobling to savor each moment as a gift from God and to spend each moment in service to God and to others. Sadly, it is a struggle which all too many people lose. Some, like Lanie, simply surrender.

As followers of Jesus Christ, we are called to imitate his quest to live life to the deepest and the fullest. His last tortured breaths, drawn as he hung upon the cross, were spent in ministry to others—forgiving his tormentors, giving assurance of salvation to the repentant thief, and assigning John to care for his bereaved mother Mary. Jesus set us an example so we could learn to live the noble struggle of life without surrendering to its pain. In him we see the beauty and dignity of a life lived courageously, lovingly, and unselfishly.

I've known many people who have struggled with deep depression. Sadly, I've lost a few of these friends to suicide. Some took their lives in the irrational belief that by doing so they would somehow do friends and family a favor. Others considered death an alternative to failing health, the shame of scandal, or the loss of a career and financial security. The impulse to flee from pain rather than fight the good fight for life is not hard to understand. Yet I am reminded of the words of William Faulkner, "If I had to choose between pain and nothing, I would always choose pain." Faulkner's words are a courageous shout of defiance in the face of death and despair, the enemies of the human spirit. There is nothing in this world more fragile—and more precious—than the gift of life. This gift from God must always be cherished, never wasted.

Depression is a dark and dimly understood component of the human condition. More than just a case of the blues or a touch of melancholy, true depression is in fact a psychological, emotional, and spiritual condition that plumbs the depths of the human soul. Depression blinds our judgment, chokes our joy, paralyzes our will, and defeats our spirit.

The depressed person finds himself going through a bewildering array of emotional changes. He doesn't want to get out of bed in the morning. He stops caring about himself and others. He finds it increasingly difficult to concentrate, to remember, and to make decisions. All the pleasures of life—friends, food, fun, and sex—seem to lose their allure. He isolates himself and is preoccupied with morbid thoughts. It's hard to fall asleep at night, hard to stay awake during the day, and impossible to be enthusiastic about anything at anytime. Physical symptoms set in: exhaustion, vague pains, queasiness, and digestive disorders. Hope fades and gloom covers everything.

Those who have never sunk to the depths of depression have difficulty understanding the pain of the truly depressed person. They are usually the ones who make insensitive comments like: "I'm sick and tired of seeing you mope around!" "You wouldn't feel that way if you'd just get right with God!" "Why don't you pull yourself together and quit feeling sorry for yourself!" "If you're trying to get sympathy from me, forget it!" But if depressed people are to find healing and a new beginning, attitudes like these will never help. The depressed person needs a lot of patience, understanding, and caring.

There are many causes of depression. Some forms are more easily alleviated than others. There is depression brought on by fatigue and stress, often called "burnout." In his book on the subject, Dr. Herbert Freudenberger offers this definition of burnout: "To deplete oneself. To exhaust one's physical and mental resources. To wear oneself out by excessively striving to reach some unrealistic expectation imposed by oneself or by the values of society."[1]

The fatigue/stress/burnout syndrome of depression is characterized by waning happiness, enthusiasm, and sensitivity to others. A victim of burnout often seems outwardly aloof and unemotional, but churns inwardly with anger, resentment, and feelings of being obstructed in life.

Some causes of burnout can be readily identified and treated. A "burned out" person can often step back, take stock of his or her life, and make positive changes based on the answers to some important questions:

Are my ambitions and goals unreasonable?

Do I need to learn how better to manage stress?

How long has it been since my last vacation?

Do I allow others to make unreasonable demands on me?

Am I getting enough rest, exercise, and nutrition?

Do I need to make some changes in my work or my life-style?

Do I let go of job-related problems when I get home?

Do I have enough outside interests to help me put my job-related problems into perspective?

Is there unresolved anger or resentment in my life?

Do I have a support group with whom I can honestly share my feelings?

But burnout often signals a deeper problem. For example, a burned out person may be obsessed with reaching an unreachable goal to compensate for a poor self-image. People who compete with themselves are bound to lose the race. Or the burned out person may be operating on the assumption that he or she is indestructible. Such people keep pushing themselves to the brink of exhaustion—and sometimes they push *beyond* the brink. They go down in flames, crash, and burn out.

Depression can often be traced to physiological causes such as unbalanced diet, exhaustion and overwork, insomnia, drug reactions, or hormonal imbalances. Thus it is always important for the depressed person to be evaluated medically. If your physician determines that your depression has no medical solution, you can begin to deal with the psychological, emotional, and spiritual dimensions of your problem.

This brings us to those forms of depression which are the most painful, destructive, and deeply entrenched. The severely depressed person is usually struggling with one or more of five basic hurts: (1) unresolved issues from the past; (2) depressive family environment; (3) major loss or grief; (4) obsessive perfectionism; or (5) unresolved guilt. Let's investigate each hurt separately.

The hurt of unresolved issues involves feelings of inferiority, resentment, and mistrust resulting from past events or patterns which reach out and stab at us in the present. I know of one businessman, for example, who continually pushed himself to work more than 70 hours per week. Though he was already wealthy and respected, he could never experience joy or contentment. He suffered deep depression even as he accumulated success upon success. Why? Because he had been repeatedly told by his father that he was a "bum" and that he would never amount to anything. He lived his life in a desperate, futile scramble to prove his father wrong—even though his father had been dead for over ten years.

Second, the hurt of a depressive family environment affects people who are preyed upon by destructive family members. Such destructive personalities use a variety of tactics, both verbal and nonverbal, to control, hurt, and exact a perverse kind of satisfaction from their victims. As a result, these victims become prone to severe depression. Because he is manipulated by someone else, the depressed person sees himself as powerless and ineffectual. He feels he only exists in the shadow of the manipulative family member. His self-image is distorted by the criticism and guilt heaped upon him in a destructive effort to subdue and control him.

Destructive people choke off communication in the home, using silence as a weapon against other family members. The victims, in turn, are unable to express their feelings—and their anger turns inward and becomes depression. A destructive parent may show favoritism, playing one child against another and encouraging the kind of rivalry that destroys a healthy self-image. The depressed person is made to feel insecure by "double-bind" messages that are superficially positive but undermined by negative facial expressions, actions, and tone of voice. "Of course I love you!" the parent barks gruffly. "Would I put up with all your annoying habits and stupid mistakes if I didn't love you?"

Third, the hurt of loss or grief is a very common cause of depression. I experienced very intense depression after the deaths of my father and my brother. Some people experience this kind of depression from losing a career, a reputation, a romance or marriage, major financial holdings, or secure and familiar surroundings, such as moving away from the family home.

Fourth, the hurt of obsessive perfectionism is rooted in a poor self-image. Such people want to be perfect and live in an orderly world. Outwardly they seem poised, controlled, organized, and unemotional. Inwardly, however, they are frightened and insecure. They continually compare themselves to unreasonable standards to see if they measure up in beauty, competence, prestige, and achievement. Such rigid perfectionists seem to set themselves up for inevitable depression. If their world proves flawed, or if they fail to meet their own standards of perfection, they say to themselves, "I'm a failure; I can't do anything well; I'm no good."

On the other hand, perfectionists who succeed in reaching their goals often find them hollow. Their achievements are not grand enough, so the race for perfection starts over again. Real joy and satisfaction are always just out of reach, while depression hovers all too near.

Fifth, the hurt of unresolved guilt is not only rooted in a poor self-image, but also in an inaccurate God-image. The guilt-ridden depressed person will ask God to forgive the same sin hundreds of times—and still never feel forgiven. His problem is not that he has neglected to confess his sin, but that he *perpetually* confesses it. A sin that God has already forgiven, forgotten, and buried in the deepest sea is

still, for this individual, very much in the present-tense,
blocking his joy and blotting out God's love for him.

Lanie was a deeply depressed young woman long before
she jumped from the Golden Gate Bridge. In fact, she suffered to some degree from all five areas of emotional hurt.

I learned about Lanie's suicide from her pastor, counselor,
and friend, who is also a good friend of mine. While she was
alive, Lanie found it difficult to articulate the pain that so
deeply troubled her. But her death speaks clearly about
depression, self-worth, and both the strength and the fra-
gility of the human spirit in a crisis of pain and insecurity.
Here is Lanie's story as shared by her pastor:

I met Lanie and her husband Alan in March 1987 when
they came to me for marriage counseling. Though they loved
each other, Lanie and Alan were driven and insecure people
who could not seem to stop hurting each other. Their deterio-
rating marriage was marked by anger, bitterness, and lack of
communication.

Lanie, who was a full time registered nurse in a large
hospital, struck me as especially insecure. She was harshly
critical of Alan, yet she was also very childlike—delicate,
sensitive, eager to please, with a wistful longing for happiness. In appearance and demeanor, Lanie projected a sense of
confidence, poise, control, and perfection. In all her roles—
health care professional, mother of two children, homemaker,
and churchwoman—she seemed organized, happy, competent, and gifted. But I soon learned that Lanie's outward
appearance was a stark contradiction of her inner reality.

Lanie grew up with a destructive, manipulative, emotionally abusive, alcoholic mother. As a girl, Lanie felt unloved,
unaccepted, and unable to measure up to her mother's expectations. Thus she became obsessed with perfection, achievement, and recognition. She was compulsively determined to
gain the acceptance her mother had denied her.

During our counseling sessions, Lanie became more open
about her past and present hurts, and her distorted self-

image became painfully evident. Though deeply committed to Christ, Lanie could never grasp and accept God's grace and unconditional love for her. Whenever I related that God loves us unconditionally, forgives us completely, and accepts us totally, she returned an uncomprehending expression, as if I were speaking in an unknown language. Lanie saw herself as unforgiven and, as such, could never arrive at a point of self-acceptance.

Though Lanie's depression was rooted in her poor self-image, it was compounded by the couple's move to the West Coast. When Alan was transferred, Lanie gave up a beautiful house in suburban Delaware for a downtown apartment in the city. She disliked her new surroundings and missed her friends on the East Coast.

While the counseling sessions seemed to be helping their relationship, Lanie's problem with depression intensified. Then in June she haltingly admitted the existence of a dark secret from the past which haunted her with guilt. At first she wouldn't tell me what her secret was, and Alan didn't know any more than I did. But I knew Lanie's secret was at the heart of her depression.

Finally in July, only days before her suicide, Lanie disclosed her secret to Alan and me. Earlier in the year, Lanie had been plagued by insomnia and tension for a couple of weeks. One night near the end of her late shift at the hospital, she went to the drug cabinet, unlocked it, and took one sedative tablet to relieve her stress. Though it's not unusual for some nurses to pocket prescription drugs for their own use, yet in her entire nursing career, Lanie had never taken anything until she took this one pill. No one ever found out, but dark guilt began to grow inside Lanie like a cancer.

Was it possible that a woman could be so paralyzed with fear, guilt, and anxiety over one little pill? Yet it was true. For various reasons—most of them imaginary—she believed herself to be a failure as a wife, mother, homemaker, and Christian. There was only one compartment of her life where she felt competent, useful, successful, and appreciated: her nursing career. But when she took that pill she violated a rigid, self-imposed rule of ethical perfection. The theft of a single pill completely shattered the only part of her life that gave her a sense of worth and self-respect. And it was the theft of that pill that finally tilted her toward suicide.

In time I think Lanie might have accepted her past hurts and discovered the reality of God's unconditional love and forgiveness. She might have gained healing insights into her painful relationship with her mother. But at this point in her life she was unable to shake her irrational certainty that she was a failure as a nurse, that she would soon be discovered, and that her career would be ruined. To Lanie, the theft of the pill proved that her mother had been right all along: she was no good.

Her depression was so intense that I suspected she might attempt suicide, but she was adamant that she could never do such a thing. We made a covenant that she could call me if she ever thought about taking her life. Yet she had come to see herself as being in the way, as a "poison" to others around her. In the deep places of her soul, she tragically concluded that her death would be the best thing for everyone.

Lanie planned her suicide with characteristic competence, thoroughness, and perfection. Unknown to her husband, she organized her financial affairs, updated her will, and made provisions for the distribution of her personal effects and cherished mementos. She had her hair and nails done. Her dress, earrings, and makeup had been carefully chosen.

The morning of her death, she was uncharacteristically cheerful and upbeat. A friend who had been concerned about her long bout with depression noticed her new mood that morning and mistakenly concluded that Lanie had finally turned the corner on her depression. Actually, Lanie had simply arrived at a place of peace with her tragic decision.

I believe suicide is a sin, but it is not the unforgivable sin. The tragedy of Lanie's suicide is that it was a permanent solution to a temporary problem—a problem that would have eventually yielded to patient, diligent effort in counseling.

There are lots of people in the world like Lanie. They tell themselves, as she did, "If others really knew me, they could never accept me. Even God could never love someone like me." Those who wrestle with the same impulses that propelled Lanie to her death are locked away from joy, fellowship with God, and fellowship with others. They need to be understood and accepted. They need to have people around them who will love them until they are able to love themselves.

I believe God grieves over the pain that we feel in the throes of depression. "The LORD is close to the brokenhearted," says Psalm 34:18, "and saves those who are crushed in spirit." The God of a new beginning is close to you right now, and he wants to bring you to a place of healing and joy. "I have come that they may have life," Jesus said in John 10:10, "and have it to the full."

There are several specific actions you can take to find the full, abundant life beyond depression. Set aside daily time to reflect on your life and the Scriptures. Ask yourself, "What kinds of thinking patterns tend to lead me into depression? Have I become focused on self-pity, bitterness, or resentment?" Replace these thoughts with thankfulness to God and recognition of all the blessings he brings into your life.

Re-examine your negative assumptions. Upon reflection, you may realize that the mistake you made is really not the end of the world, or that the person who made that insensitive remark was really not out to get you. In his book, *Now I Know Why I'm Depressed (And What I Can Do About It)*, Dr. H. Norman Wright observes, "When we become depressed we tend to do less and think more negatively, which in turn creates more depression . . . . We feel frustrated and blocked, and possibly self-pity sets in as well. All of these thoughts and emotions then lead to the intensification of yet another feeling—loss of control and further loss of self-esteem. All of this deepens our depression."[2] By deliberately choosing a positive interpretation of your life circumstances, you can break the vicious cycle of your depression.

Don't allow your life-style to sink with your moods. Determine to keep a regular schedule of activity, even when you don't feel like it. Don't lose touch with friends. Don't let dirty dishes stack up in the sink. Don't stay in bed or phone in sick to the office. Maintain your routine, but take an occasional break from work. Get out of the office or the house for a few minutes and take a brisk walk. Exercise is important. Studies show that exercise propels mood-lifting oxygen to the brain and releases anti-depressant chemicals such as catecholamines and endorphins into the bloodstream.

Find a trusted friend with whom you can honestly share your feelings, someone you can trust to listen without judging. If people try to help you out of your depression in inappropriate ways, be frank with them. Tell them that it doesn't make you feel any better to be kidded, cajoled, or scolded. Tell them that you appreciate their concern for you and would be glad to receive their prayer, encouragement, and authentic support.

Always remember: *depression is temporary*. No matter how bad things seem, no matter how serious your depression, it will pass.

If you feel down on yourself, worthless, and unforgiven, reflect on where your focus is. Are you focused on yourself, your sin, and your mistakes? Or are you focused on the goodness, grace, and unconditional love of God? Remember, you are a child of your loving Father. You are made in His image. You are an heir of the riches of His grace. Make His forgiveness—not your blame—your focus.

Don't hesitate to seek biblically-based counseling from your pastor or a professional counselor. Pastoral counseling is free of charge. And if professional counseling is needed, many churches have a fund to defray counseling fees so you can get the help you need.

Life is hard and depression hurts. But there is joy and nobility in a life lived honestly, courageously, and faithfully to God. The apostle Paul knew that. He wrote in 2 Corinthians 4:8-10: "We are hard pressed on every side, but not crushed; perplexed, but not in despair; persecuted, but not abandoned; struck down, but not destroyed. We always carry around in our body the death of Jesus, so that the life of Jesus may also be revealed in our body."

The life of Jesus is revealed in us not as we die in despair, but as we authentically *live* for him and journey with hope and courage toward the new beginning he has created for us. I pray that God will lift you up from the deep places of your soul and into the light of his infinite love. May you truly *live* all the days of your life, and may you find perfect joy and peace in the presence of our loving Father at a time of his own choosing.

15

Prone to Wander

It was a bright Sunday morning in 18th century London, but Robert Robinson's mood was anything but sunny. All along the street there were people hurrying to church, but in the midst of the crowd Robinson was a lonely man. The sound of church bells reminded him of years past when his faith in God was strong and the church was an integral part of his life. It had been years since he set foot in a church—years of wandering, disillusionment, and gradual defection from the God he once loved. That love for God—once fiery and passionate—had slowly burned out within him, leaving him dark and cold inside.

Robinson heard the *clip-clop, clip-clop* of a horse-drawn cab approaching behind him. Turning, he lifted his hand to hail the driver. But then he saw that the cab was occupied by a young woman dressed in finery for the Lord's Day. He waved the driver on, but the woman in the carriage ordered the carriage to be stopped.

"Sir, I'd be happy to share this carriage with you," she said to Robinson. "Are you going to church?"

Robinson was about to decline, then he paused. "Yes," he said at last. "I am going to church." He stepped into the carriage and sat down beside the young woman.

As the carriage rolled forward Robert Robinson and the woman exchanged introductions. There was a flash of recognition in her eyes when he stated his name. "That's an interesting coincidence," she said, reaching into her purse. She withdrew a small book of inspirational verse, opened it to a ribbon-bookmark, and handed the book to him. "I was just reading a verse by a poet named Robert Robinson. Could it be . . . ?"

He took the book, nodding. "Yes, I wrote these words years ago."

"Oh, how wonderful!" she exclaimed. "Imagine! I'm sharing a carriage with the author of these very lines!"

But Robinson barely heard her. He was absorbed in the words he was reading. They were words that would one day be set to music and become a great hymn of the faith, familiar to generations of Christians:

> Come, Thou Fount of every blessing,
> Tune my heart to sing Thy grace;
> Streams of mercy, never ceasing,
> Call for songs of loudest praise.

His eyes slipped to the bottom of the page where he read:

> Prone to wander, Lord, I feel it—
> Prone to leave the God I love;
> Here's my heart, O take and seal it,
> Seal it for Thy courts above.

He could barely read the last few lines through the tears that brimmed in his eyes. "I wrote these words—and I've lived these words. 'Prone to wander . . . prone to leave the God I love.' "

The woman suddenly understood. "You also wrote, 'Here's my heart, O take and seal it.' You *can* offer your heart again to God, Mr. Robinson. It's not too late."

And it wasn't too late for Robert Robinson. In that moment he turned his heart back to God and walked with him the rest of his days.

I identify with Robert Robinson. Like him, I know in my heart that I am prone to wander, prone to defect, prone to leave the God I love. Perhaps you identify with Robert Robinson as well. Somewhere during your Christian journey, your faith became less real and less vital to you. Your prayer life dried up. You feel like you're just going through the motions of the Christian life. You remember mornings when you led your family in devotions. You remember nights in bed with your spouse, holding hands and taking turns sharing your thoughts, joys, and concerns aloud with God. But these are just memories now. Gradually and subtly you have wandered.

Perhaps you feel you are missing something that the world has to offer. People around you seem to be getting ahead in the world. They make a lot of money and get a lot of recognition. They live immoral lives without seeming to pay a price. Meanwhile you try to be diligent and honest at your job, involved in your church, and upright in your life-style. Yet your life seems increasingly pointless and unrewarding. You feel burned out—and you crave the things of the world. Perhaps you haven't sinned greatly—yet. But deep in your heart you know you are wandering.

Maybe you feel stressed out in your marriage. There is increasing conflict and you and your spouse are not handling it well. The word *divorce* hangs like an unspoken threat or flashes like a weapon in every argument. You once made a vow before God that could not be broken by anything except death. But your desire to fulfil that vow is waning. You haven't committed adultery and you haven't come to the point of divorce. Yet in your marriage commitment, you have begun to wander.

Or perhaps you are weary in a position of church leadership—an elder, a deacon, a Sunday school teacher. You remember the joy that Christian service once brought you. But the years of hectic schedules, long meetings, and petty church politics and infighting have left you disillusioned. Your faith has taken a beating. You're sick of it all. You want out. You feel yourself wandering.

It happens so slowly we don't realize it. We defect, we wander. If we don't restore our spiritual vitality and love for God somehow, we will end up like Jonah, swallowed up in rebellion against God. Or maybe we'll end up like Peter, denying Christ and betraying our love for him.

Years ago I was the Bible teacher for the Minnesota Vikings football team. I saw a number of players make commitments to Jesus Christ. Many of them spoke at churches or meetings of the Fellowship of Christian Athletes (FCA), sharing before hundreds of people the difference that Jesus Christ made in their lives. If you were a football fan during those years, you would certainly know the names of these men. Some of them are still strong witnesses for Jesus Christ. But others, I'm sad to say, are not.

Initially each Christian athlete was excited about his new-found relationship with Christ. But some of these men began to wander. Fame, wealth, and the praise of the fans became more important to them than Jesus Christ. Gradually they drifted away from the FCA Bible study. Some of these men joined with other players who met in a bar and called themselves the FPA—Fellowship of Pagan Athletes—in an overt affront to Christianity. They flaunted their hard drinking, fast living, and crude humor, and scorned those who pursued a moral life-style. At one time they followed Christ. Most of them probably thought they would never wander from the faith. Then they spurned him.

Spiritual defection—do you think it could ever happen to you? If not, you may be in far more danger than you imagine! "If you think you are standing firm," warns 1 Corinthians 10:12, "be careful that you don't fall!" No one is immune to spiritual defection—*no one*. One of my greatest fears is that, after having counseled and preached and written books about how to have a richer love-relationship with God, I might wander, I might defect. "Prone to wander," wrote Robert Robinson, "Lord, I feel it." I do feel it. And I fear it.

I believe the fear of wandering is an honest, healthy fear. We *should* be afraid of losing our love for God. Not terrified, not paralyzed, not trembling with fear, but honestly concerned and vigilant. We should examine ourselves regularly and recognize our propensity for sin and defection.

How can you learn to guard yourself against spiritual defection? First, make integrity the central pillar of your character. The dictionary defines integrity as "an adherence to a code of moral values; the quality of being undivided and honest." But there's more to it than that, isn't there? Integrity means being morally pure even in the small, insignificant things. Integrity means being pure even when no one is watching. Integrity means being pure even when there is a price to pay for purity.

When I think of integrity, I think of a conversation I had with a young Christian leader in his early twenties who was preparing to give his life to full-time Christian service. I asked him what was the most important factor in his commitment to serve and follow Jesus Christ. His answer: "My Mom and Dad—and especially their integrity. Ron, I've always been impressed by the fact that my parents lived exactly what they said they believed." If there is anyone in the world who watches our lives and knows whether we live with integrity or not, it is our children. Living our lives congruently with our words is a powerful witness to our children.

Not long ago, I was surprised to learn that a friend of mine, a Christian businessman I have greatly respected over the years, took advantage of some of the privileges of his position. His company gave him an expense account to be used in connection with his work. Yet on a couple of occasions he used that expense account to take his wife out to dinner. He also charged a couple of personal pleasure trips on his expense account.

Integrity means that if your employer were to investigate you, he would not find even one of the company's paper clips in your pocket. If we learn to keep our walk pure in the small things, we will be true, faithful, and incorruptible in the important things.

If you think you are a person of integrity, consider these questions: Do you ever shade the truth or tell "little white lies"? If you are given too much change at the supermarket, do you give it back? Have you ever "fudged" on your income tax return—just a little? Is your behavior as blameless and upright when you are alone as when others are watching you? Did you ever make photocopies at work or at church without paying for them? If telling the truth would cost you a thousand dollars, would you tell a lie? Did you ever decide to do something after asking yourself, "Who would it really hurt if I just—"?

I don't think anyone ever chooses suddenly, precipitously to rebel against God or to commit a gross and terrible sin. Spiritual defection is an imperceptibly gradual process made up of hundreds of small, seemingly insignificant choices which slowly lead us away from God. As C.S. Lewis observed in *The Screwtape Letters*, "The safest road to Hell is the gradual one—the gentle slope, soft underfoot, without sudden turnings, without milestones, without signposts."[1] That's the process we follow when we give in to temptation in those seemingly minor areas. The cumulative effect of all those "minor" sins is devastating. Ultimately, we find ourselves so far from God we can no longer see him or hear his voice. Then, when a great temptation comes, we fall to it—and often it is a resounding, humiliating fall.

We are prone to wander. We know that Romans 12:1 urges us to present ourselves as a living sacrifice to God. But the problem with a living sacrifice is that it keeps crawling off the altar! To be a living sacrifice means that we commit ourselves daily to a life-style of integrity whether the issues are small or large, whether someone is watching or not, and whether it costs us nothing or everything.

A second way to guard against spiritual defection is to make yourself accountable to other Christians. Accountability is the process of voluntarily opening one's life to the scrutiny of others through mutual questioning and counseling. Accountability is a key ingredient in my own spiritual, mental, and emotional growth. It has been a central part of my journey toward Christlikeness.

The book of Proverbs is filled with passages which call us to mutual accountability: "Pride only breeds quarrels, but wisdom is found in those who take advice" (13:10); "He who listens to a life-giving rebuke will be at home among the wise" (15:31); and one of my favorites, "As iron sharpens iron, so one man sharpens another" (27:17). I am learning from the Scriptures and from my daily walk with Christ that I need the counsel of a few friends who love me enough to question me, offer suggestions, and lend me their insight. I need to be in a relationship of mutual accountability with Christian brothers and sisters who have earned the right to be heard by their affirmation, acceptance, and unconditional love for me.

Cal Thomas, syndicated columnist and radio commentator, was interviewed in *Discipleship Journal* on the subject of accountability. As a journalist, Thomas has viewed scores of moral tragedies, from political scandals to Wall Street scams to the public humiliation of popular religious figures. He observes that, whether we are rich and famous or just plain folk, accountability is essential to keeping ourselves from spiritual defection. He notes:

> Regardless of our role or status, we need to be accountable to others who lovingly ask us hard questions about our goals and motivations and hold us true to our faith in Jesus Christ.... One of the best ways I know is through small groups. To be truly accountable requires honesty and vulnerability. This usually happens most effectively within a small group where people have made commitments to one another and established trust. In this

setting we are best able to give someone permission
to ask us the hard questions and challenge us on
our inconsistencies . . . . Each of us needs that small
group of Christians who love us, pray for us, know
us, encourage us, correct us—who help us remain
true in our pursuit of the godly life.[2]

The kind of accountability Cal Thomas describes has been
an essential part of my life for years. I have made it a point to
be closely involved with several trusted Christian friends—
studying the Scriptures together, praying together, sharing
the hurts and joys of our lives with one another, and mutually
holding each other accountable. Sometimes I was part of a
"house church," a small Bible study group sponsored by our
church. Sometimes I gathered with a few Christian men
before breakfast once a week. Sometimes my accountability
group was the church staff which met weekly in a shared
bond of faith, fellowship, and ministry. But I don't dare go a
week without having people around me to observe my life,
pray for me, encourage me, and correct me when I begin to
wander.

In a relationship of mutual accountability, we can ask our
Christian brothers and sisters to help us set and meet personal goals. The areas of goal accountability can include
spiritual growth, physical discipline, organizing time and
tasks, or conquering bad habits. It's a common-sense fact of
life that behavior that is observed changes. Each of us needs
to be letting that kind of light into our lives, because no one is
immune to the seduction of this world.

Some Christians are afraid to become authentic and vulnerable before others because they may appear weak or
flawed. Such fear keeps us shrouded in darkness, rendering
us especially susceptible to defection. "But if we walk in the
light, as he [God] is in the light," says 1 John 1:7, "we have
fellowship with one another, and the blood of Jesus, his Son,
purifies us from every sin." To "walk in the light" means
becoming transparent to a few trusted friends, allowing the

light of their Spirit-led discernment and love to penetrate
our lives.

Walking in the light produces "fellowship with one another."
Fellowship provides a safe refuge where we are free to be real
and honest with our friends. In the light of mutual fellowship
we are accepted, affirmed, and encouraged no matter how far
we have fallen or how deeply we are hurting. Most important
of all, walking in the light means that the purifying blood of
Jesus is powerfully at work in our lives as we confess our
humanness, fallibility, and sin to one another.

One of the greatest affirmations you can receive is to hear
a Christian brother or sister tell you sincerely, "I've watched
your life in these past months and I've seen you grow. You're
becoming more and more like Christ." If you don't hear words
like these, perhaps it's because you are living in a state of
isolation rather than a state of mutual accountability with
other believers.

Mary was a fresh-faced, squeaky-clean Christian young
woman full of winsome, effervescent joy that immediately
charmed everyone she met. She and her friends Peggy and
Beth, who were also outgoing Christians, found employment
together in a large office in southern California. All three
women were very frank about their faith and never missed
an opportunity during lunch or coffee breaks to talk to others
about Jesus Christ.

Mary gained many friends in the office, including a handsome young executive named Ted. Sensing a romantic notion
in Mary, Peggy took her friend aside. "Do you realize that Ted
is married and has three little children?" she asked.

Mary was shaken. "No, he never mentioned it," she answered. Mary seemed hurt for a few moments. Then suddenly
her face hardened. "You know, Peggy," she said, "it's really
none of your business what I do with my life, is it?" Mary's
message to her friend was, in effect, "I'm not accountable to
you or anyone else for my actions."

Mary became deeply involved with Ted. Her flirtation
with him turned into an affair. Peggy and Beth took Mary

out to lunch one day and confronted her lovingly about her life-style. They reminded her about the hurt she was causing herself, her illicit lover, and his family.

Mary sat in stony silence during their lunch together. But when her friends offered to pray with her, she jumped angrily to her feet. "No!" she shouted. "This is my life! You have no right to interfere with *my* life!" Mary stormed out of the restaurant and for weeks afterward she avoided her Christian friends. In the meantime, Ted left his wife and moved into Mary's apartment.

One day at the office, Mary was disciplined by her supervisor for an error in her work. When Ted heard about it, he cornered the supervisor in the lunchroom, grabbed him by the lapels, and shouted, "I'm warning you! Hassle Mary one more time and you're dead! You understand? Dead!" At the end of the day, Ted was told to clean out his desk, pick up his final check, and never return.

Months later, Ted was still jobless and living off of Mary's salary. He became increasingly sullen and abusive, but Mary was sure he would be all right once the divorce finalized and he found a new job. During the divorce proceedings, Ted's wife claimed he had frequently beaten her and threatened to kill her. "She's lying," Ted assured Mary smoothly. "She'll say anything to get even with me for leaving her."

After the divorce, Mary and Ted were married. But the marriage started to disintegrate almost as soon as it began. Ted quit looking for work and drank heavily during the day. The couple fought incessantly, and several times Ted struck Mary. Scared, and convinced she had no future with Ted, Mary filed for divorce and moved back to her parents' home.

Life began to brighten for Mary. She called Peggy and apologized for resisting Peggy's attempt to rescue her from her folly. "I really think my life is coming together now," Mary said hopefully.

The next day Mary was alone at her parents' home when Ted showed up with a gun, blind with rage. He kicked the door open and dragged Mary into the front yard. She screamed and struggled, but Ted shoved the gun into her ribs and fired, fatally wounding her. Then he turned the gun on himself.

How could Mary have imagined that her romantic notions toward a married man would result in a murder-suicide? Somehow this vibrant Christian young woman slipped into a pattern of rebellion and adultery. She defected, she drifted, and she spurned the loving attempts of her friends to bring her back. Mary's decision to remain unaccountable cost her unspeakable pain and, ultimately, her life.

Earlier in my ministry, when I was serving in another church, I became concerned that some in our congregation were overly absorbed with minute details of Bible prophecy, such as the symbolism of the Beast and the exact schedule of the Second Coming of Christ. A class on prophecy, taught by a godly man I deeply respected, attracted many members. This rapt fascination with prophetic events troubled me.

One Sunday as I stepped into the pulpit to preach, I chose a Scripture text outlining our mission as Christians to demonstrate compassion for the poor and hungry. In the course of my message, I made a statement which I considered to be a bold and biblical challenge to the congregation: "It would be well if some of us were as concerned for the hungry children of the world as we are about learning every detail about the Second Coming of Jesus Christ."

The next morning I received a call from a very special and beloved friend in the church. He made an appointment to meet me for lunch the following Wednesday. When we met, he spoke humbly and gently, but frankly—not to tear me down, but to build me up and make me a better man for Christ.

"You know, Ron," he began, "I think you could have raised the point about our responsibility to the poor and hungry just as strongly without setting it against an interest in Bible prophecy. I know you didn't mean to, but I think you put the teacher of the prophecy class in a bad light. I haven't talked to him, but my hunch is that he was probably hurt by what you said. I encourage you to talk to him."

I took my friend's advice and contacted the teacher. I asked him how he felt about what I said in my sermon. In a very gracious way he told me that my remarks about prophecy had hurt him. I apologized to him and reconciled with him. It was a painful moment in my life, but it was a pivotal moment in my ministry. It brought change and growth to my life. I made a commitment then to be very precise and careful whenever I opened the Word of God in the pulpit. I promised God that I would never use the pulpit as a hammer, or approach a sermon with a hidden agenda or an axe to grind. I believe any pastor who does use the pulpit in that way disgraces the Word of God. I know there are pastors who do so— and I believe the reason they do so is that a lot of pastors don't have a caring friend like this friend of mine who gently but firmly held me accountable.

We need accountability. I need it, and so do you.

The third way to guard against spiritual defection is perhaps the most important. And in view of the fallibility of human flesh, it may also be the hardest to do: *Learn how to deal with temptation*. And that's another chapter.

16

Deliver Us from Evil

Gordon MacDonald tells the story of a Christian executive friend of his who frequently traveled far from home on business. Having concluded a day's business on one of his trips, the executive decided to take a walk near his downtown hotel.

Not too far from his hotel he came upon a pornographic movie theater. He had never attended such a theater or even so much as purchased a *Playboy* magazine before. But a curiosity aroused by the skulking brute called *lust*, which always seems to lurk at the threshold of the male mind, prompted him to stop and examine the marquee. He stood staring at the posters on the marquee for a moment. Then he looked up and down the street. *You're far from home in a strange city,* he thought. *Who will ever know?*

Almost before he realized it the decision was made. He reached into his pocket, pulled out his money, and stepped to the ticket booth. Suddenly a line from a hymn came to his mind—or could it have been the gentle urging of God's Spirit? "I would be true, for there are those who trust me. I would be pure, for there are those who care."

The man in the ticket-booth frowned as he folded his money and put it back in his pocket. "Never mind," he said, and he turned and walked back to his hotel room.

You and I are not always as successful in our struggle with temptation are we? This man's temptation was in the area of sexual lust. But temptation assails us in many forms and from many directions. We are tempted to join our culture in worldly expressions of ambition, greed, and revenge. We are tempted to lust for power, recognition, and material possessions. We are tempted to overindulge our appetites for food, alcohol, or drugs. The list goes on and on.

Temptation is a powerful enemy. It begins with a brief, fleeting thought. Then the thought returns. And if we allow it to stay, it will haunt and entice us. We find ourselves wondering, "What am I missing out on? Maybe I'll try it— maybe not." The next time the thought occurs, we leave off "maybe not." We teeter on the brink of a decision, flirting with the wrong choice. Soon the decision to commit sin is made even before we are fully aware of it.

Temptation is not sin. Temptation attacks us from the outside. It's always around us and always will be. Yet all along, at every step of the way, it is our choice either to invite temptation to stay or to forcibly eject it from our lives.

In Matthew 4 we see that even Jesus was surrounded by temptation. Alone in the desert, weak and hungry from a 40-day fast, Jesus faced a level of temptation beyond our comprehension. But he faced it successfully. As Hebrews 4:15 tells us, Jesus was "tempted in every way, just as we are—yet was without sin." Whatever temptation you face, no matter how irresistible and insurmountable you think it is, Jesus has faced it—and won! You can win too.

Sometimes we think of Jesus only in his role as the Son of God—deity. We see him as distant, exalted, and untouched by our human frailties. But remember, the Bible also calls Jesus the Son of Man—a human being. As man, he was touched by pain, need, and temptation just as we are. By some means which is beyond our understanding, Jesus was both fully God and fully man. As the eternal God, Jesus clothed himself in the flesh and blood of humanity. He endured temptation—not to make us feel morally inferior, but to encourage us and be an example to us. Jesus is the proof that you and I can live victoriously over temptation, even within the limited confines of the human condition. As the apostle Paul assures us in 1 Corinthians 10:13, "No temptation has seized you except what is common to man. And God is faithful; he will not let you be tempted beyond what you can bear. But when you are tempted, he will also provide a way out so that you can stand up under it."

In the example Jesus left us, we see that he conquered temptation in several ways. First, Jesus kept his eyes on God the Father. When Satan tempted him, Jesus replied with a statement demonstrating that his focus was on God, not his circumstances. He said, in Matthew 4:4, "It is written: 'Man does not live on bread alone, but on every word that comes from the mouth of God.'" Then in 4:7, Jesus stated, "It is also written: 'Do not put the Lord your God to the test.'" And in 4:10 he said, "It is written: 'Worship the Lord your God, and serve him only.'"

In his insightful book, *Temptation*, Dietrich Bonhoeffer observes that we become vulnerable to sinful desire when we take our eyes off of God and seek our joy in anything except the desire for God himself. Bonhoeffer writes:

> In our members there is a slumbering inclination towards desire which is both sudden and fierce. With irresistible power desire seizes mastery over the flesh. All at once a secret, smoldering fire is kindled. The flesh burns and is in flames. It makes no difference whether it is sexual desire, or ambition, or vanity, or desire for revenge, or love of fame and power, or greed for money ... Joy in God [becomes] extinguished in us and we seek all our joy in [that temptation]. At this moment, God is quite

160 Deliver Us from Evil

> unreal to us, he loses all reality, and only desire for
> the [temptation] is real...Satan does not [in a
> moment of temptation] fill us with hatred of God,
> but with forgetfulness of God.[1]

Bonhoeffer is right. When Satan assails us with temptation, he does so with craft and subtlety. He doesn't try anything so overt and obvious as to make us hate God. He just wants us to forget God for awhile. Thus, by keeping our eyes focused on God we guard ourselves from temptation.

My friend Elton Gillam poses some questions that I have found helpful whenever I feel tempted to forget God. He asks, "Where is your gaze? And where is your glance? Is your gaze focused on God? Or do you merely glance at God while you gaze on your circumstances, your problems, your wants, and your desires?" Jesus' circumstances were loneliness, hunger, and persistent temptation by Satan. In his humanness, Jesus surely desired comfort, food, and a place to rest among friends. Yet he chose to only glance at his circumstances while keeping his gaze upon God the Father—and he won the battle against temptation. So can we.

Second, Jesus was able to conquer temptation because he knew the Scriptures and used them as a defense against temptation. When Satan tempted Jesus in the desert, Jesus replied again and again, "It is written." Jesus dramatically demonstrated the words of Paul in 2 Timothy 3:16-17: "All Scripture is God-breathed and is useful for teaching, rebuking, correcting and training in righteousness, so that the man of God may be thoroughly equipped for every good work." If we neglect to build the Word of God into our lives, we set ourselves up for failure. But if we have a solid foundation in the Word of God, we are thoroughly equipped to withstand temptation.

Third, Jesus was able to conquer temptation because he rejected temptation instantly and with total finality. He didn't stop to ponder any alternatives. He didn't say, "Give me time to think it over, Satan." He didn't pause to weigh the pros and cons. He responded swiftly and firmly to each of the three temptations Satan offered him. And the third time he punctuated his response with a command: "Away from me, Satan!" (Matthew 4:10). Satan did flee from Jesus, just as he will flee from us when we firmly and instantaneously reject temptation. James 4:7 tells us, "Resist the devil, and he will flee from you." We run into danger when we let temptation flirt with us—and we flirt back.

We live in a sensual society. There is an enormous focus today on the gratification of the senses. We chase after pleasures and experiences, and we greedily crave a taste of every flavor life has to offer. We are like children at a Baskin-Robbins ice cream counter demanding a 31-scoop cone. In our mad drive to sample every possible pleasure and experience, we sometimes yield to destructive temptations while discarding the richest pleasures and the best experiences life has to offer. In his book, *Sin: Overcoming the Ultimate Deadly Addiction*, Keith Miller describes a man who made such a choice:

> Years ago I talked to a man who had a good marriage to a lovely woman he was very fond of. But he liked to have casual affairs with younger women. When confronted with a choice, he decided to leave the marriage—even though he admitted that was stupid. He began to eat compulsively and withdrew into himself, alienating many of his former friends. He is now a sad, lonely man who is obviously destroying himself—even though he has everything he could want materially—but he still won't give up his casual sexual affairs.[2]

That is the deceitfulness of sin in operation. When tempted, our sense of reality can tilt as we desperately grasp for ways to justify our corrupt desires. The result of our tilted rationality is denial. And denial is not just a lie we tell to others. It's a lie we tell to ourselves—and earnestly begin to believe.

Denial is the ability to tell ourselves that black is white, and then to build our lives upon that falsehood.

The deceitful power of sin is so strong that none of us is immune. We are all capable of believing and living out the lies we tell ourselves. Keith Miller continues:

> Through a process called denial we can rational- ize and trick ourselves into thinking we aren't exactly transgressing our values, or that, if we are, it is actually for the good of the person we are hurting. For example, the husband I spoke of ear- lier said that being unfaithful to his spouse took the pressure off her to perform sexually. He had to deny to himself a *lot* of things he knew about her feelings and values to come up with that bizarre logic.[3]

Our desperate need in times of temptation is to penetrate the fog of sin's deception and see our truest and deepest self-interest. For our truest needs are not for the things we so easily lust after—sensual experiences, wealth, power, or pleasure. Rather our deepest needs are for the values that our lusts can steal from us—family, friendships, love, self-worth, reputation, integrity, mental health, physical health, spiri- tual wholeness, and even our souls.

In a recent interview in *Time* magazine, comedian Bill Cosby talked about a time in his life when he nearly traded the things he treasured most—his wife and children—for a tempting experience. Cosby did not describe the kind of "selfish behavior" he entertained in the late 1970s. But he did say that he deeply hurt his wife Camille by his actions. He somberly added:

> When you're younger, you want to be sure that by the time you're 80 years old you can sit on the bench and look back and say, "Man, I did it all. I didn't miss a thing." ... But then you see the look on the

face of the person you didn't mean to hurt, and then you realize that what you stand to lose is worth so much more.[4]

Cosby asked his wife and children to forgive him for his "selfish behavior." Since then he has worn a silver bracelet he bought for himself. The inscription on the bracelet reads: CAMILLE'S HUSBAND.

God calls us to be a special people in a world of sensuality and self-gratification. When we are centered on our truest values—love for God and family, personal integrity, and our wholeness as people made in the image of God—we will be equipped to withstand the seductive and destructive temptations of our age.

The story of Adam and Eve in Genesis 3 is a tragedy of failure in the face of temptation. Beguiled and seduced by the serpent, these two people made a choice which cost them paradise, cursed their lives with hardship, and imposed upon them the sentence of death.

But a few chapters later, in Genesis 39, we find a much different story—the story of a young man's victory over temptation. Joseph was a servant to an Egyptian officer named Potiphar. The temptation facing Joseph was sexual in nature: Potiphar's wife approached Joseph in an attempt to seduce him. But Joseph rejected her advances instantly and totally: "Everything he [Potiphar] owns he has entrusted to my care," he replied to the temptress. "My master has withheld nothing from me except you, because you are his wife. How then could I do such a wicked thing and sin against God?"

Notice first how Joseph kept his gaze upon God in his time of temptation. He expressed *loyalty* to his master, but he expressed *obedience* to his God. Joseph knew that if he yielded to this temptation, he would be accountable for his sin first and foremost to God.

Notice also the duration of Joseph's temptation. The seductive approach of Potiphar's wife was not just a one-time, isolated instance. Genesis 39:10 says, "And though she spoke

to Joseph day after day, he refused to go to bed with her
or even to be with her." This woman forced temptation on
Joseph—a handsome, red-blooded young man in his twenties—on a daily basis. Yet he chose to persevere in his purity.
It was a relentless battle. It would have been so easy to give
in. But he wouldn't give in.

And the reason Joseph would not give in was because he
was a young man of integrity. He demonstrated his integrity
by his loyalty to his master and to God. And Joseph's integrity proved costly. For when Potiphar's wife finally tired of
merely tempting Joseph, she took his cloak in her hand and
demanded, "Come to bed with me!" Joseph had to run from
her, leaving his cloak in her hand. So this angry and frustrated temptress, unable to lure Joseph into her bed, chose
instead to destroy him. She falsely accused him of attempted
rape and had him thrown into prison.

Throughout the story we see that Joseph was faithful to
God. He kept his integrity intact regardless of the personal
cost. Moreover, we see that God was faithful to Joseph. He
ultimately exalted Joseph, making him second-in-command
over all of Egypt. In different but equally valid ways, God is
faithful to you and me as we struggle to maintain our purity
in an impure age. You may have to pay a price in this world to
resist temptation and maintain your integrity. But God will
honor your faithfulness.

It wasn't long ago that a friend of mine, a Christian businessman named Ray, came to me with a dilemma. He said,
"Ron, my company wants me to do some things that, as a
Christian, I just can't do with a clear conscience. I'm 50 years
old and I've been with this firm for 25 years. But if I don't
play along with the big boys, I'll be out on my ear."

Ray and I prayed together about the moral decision he
faced. By the time we finished praying, Ray had made the
only decision he could make as a man of Christian integrity.
A short time later, Ray went back to his superiors and an-

nounced his decision not to comply with the company's orders. He was fired on the spot. Sometimes there is a price to pay for living a righteous life.

There may come a time when you will have to make a moral choice that will cost you your job. But at least you won't lose your integrity. You might lose some friends by making the right moral choice. But at least you won't lose your integrity. You might lose a lot of money and a more affluent life-style by making the right choice. But at least you will still have your integrity. And you will have God's approval.

In Matthew 6, Jesus gives us another important insight into dealing with temptation: prayer. In Matthew 6:13, Jesus instructed His disciples to pray, "And lead us not into temptation, but deliver us from the evil one." Dealing with temptation is a matter of prayerful vigilance. "Watch and pray so that you will not fall into temptation," Jesus told His disciples in Matthew 26:41. "The spirit is willing, but the body is weak."

When you pray for deliverance from temptation, ask God to lead you away from those areas where you know you are weak and can easily fall. I know where those areas are in my life; I'm sure you know your weaknesses as well. Be honest with God and with yourself. Name specifically the sin or habit which afflicts you and confess that weakness to God, asking for his strength to avoid it and to overcome it. When you honestly name the temptation which haunts you, you will be more likely to guard against it when it comes your way. And I think you will find it impossible to succumb to a temptation you are praying about.

After prayer comes commitment. Whatever you pray *for*, commit yourself *to*. Recognize that God can use you to answer your own prayer. While you are praying to be delivered from temptation, remove yourself from temptation's way. Replace your negative patterns and habits with positive pursuits. For example, if your present life-style frequently brings you into contact with people, influences, or activities that break down your resolve to live a pure life, then change your life-style. Redeem your spare time with positive activities. Set aside time for contemplation and personal Bible study. Join a Bible study group and read good books (use your public and church libraries). Develop hobbies, attend concerts, and join special interest groups. Get the exercise you need (you can bike, join a racquet club, or, like me, run or jog). Spend quality leisure time with your family and with Christian friends.

Then learn to repattern your thoughts. For example, if lustful thoughts are a problem for you, practice praying instead. In your prayers, don't dwell on the temptation itself. Instead, focus on thanksgiving and pray about other needs for yourself, your friends, and your family. If you are plagued by bitterness and vengeful thoughts toward another person, practice praying for that person. Learn to love that person unconditionally even when you don't feel like loving. If worldly ambition or envy is your temptation, meditate on such Bible passages as 1 Timothy 6:6-11, which promises that "godliness with contentment is great gain... For the love of money is a root of all kinds of evil. Some people, eager for money, have wandered from the faith and pierced themselves with many griefs."

Whatever your temptation, in time you can learn—with patience, practice, prayer, and persistence—to repattern your thinking. It's a matter of feeding your mind the right kind of food. As Paul said in Philippians 4:8, "Whatever is true, whatever is noble, whatever is right, whatever is pure, whatever is lovely, whatever is admirable—if anything is excellent or praiseworthy—think about such things." F.B. Meyer observes so concisely, "Sow a thought, reap an act. Sow an act, reap a habit. Sow a habit, reap your character. Sow your character, reap your destiny." Be careful that the thoughts, acts, and habits you sow are those which produce character leading to a glorious and noble destiny—not a sad end.

The Victor Hugo classic *Les Miserables* is about a man who succumbed to a momentary temptation and paid a terrible price. The protagonist, Jean Valjean, stole a loaf of bread to feed his sister's starving children. He was caught, tried, and sentenced for the theft. He spent 19 years in a dungeon for his crime.

Upon his release, he could find no employment because of his prison record. Only one man, an elderly bishop, showed compassion to Jean Valjean. The churchman took Valjean into his home, gave him food and a bed, and prayed for him. But Valjean was so desperate that he yielded to temptation again. He stole some silver plates from his host and fled into the night.

But the thief was quickly captured by the police and taken back to the house of the bishop. The police displayed the stolen silver plates to the surprised bishop and asked if they belonged to him. "Yes, they are mine," answered the bishop. "That is, I gave them to him. And Jean," the bishop added, turning his eyes to the arrested man, "you forgot to take the candlesticks." The bishop was a man who understood grace and forgiveness.

We are all tempted. We all fail. And failure in the face of temptation can exact a heavy price: sin, guilt, broken relationships, humiliation, loss of integrity, loss of self-worth, and spiritual defection. But failure in the face of temptation does not need to be the end. Like the bishop in Victor Hugo's story, God is always ready to forgive us and restore us.

Temptation is our enemy, but it does not have to be our master. God the Father is our Master. If we keep our gaze upon him, he will lead us out of temptation and he will deliver us from evil.

17

Becoming Intimate
with the Infinite

After fleeing Hitler's Germany in the late 1930s, Albert Einstein found refuge in America. He purchased a quaint, old two-story house on a tree-lined street within walking distance of Princeton University. There the world's foremost mathematician entertained some of the most distinguished scientific and political personalities of the age. He discussed with his noted guests the issues which intrigued his celebrated mind—from physics to religion to human rights. Many of the great ideas which have shaped our modern world were conceived behind the green shutters of that modest little house.

But Einstein had another frequent visitor in his home. She was not a physicist or a world leader. She was a ten-year-old girl named Emmy.

Emmy heard that a very kind man who knew a lot about mathematics had moved into her neighborhood. Since Emmy was having some difficulty with her fifth-grade arithmetic, she decided to visit the man down the block and see if he would help her with her problems. Einstein was very willing and he explained everything to her so that she could easily

understand it. He also told her she was welcome to come and
knock on his front door whenever she encountered a problem
that was too difficult.

A few weeks later, Emmy's mother learned from one of her
neighbors that Emmy was often seen entering the house of
the world-famous physicist. When she asked Emmy about it,
the girl admitted it was so. "Why, Emmy!" the mother exclaimed. "Professor Einstein is a very important man! His
time is very valuable! He can't be bothered with the problems
of a little schoolgirl."

Then Emmy's mother rushed over to Einstein's house and
knocked on the door. When Einstein answered the door, she
was so flustered at the sight of the famous lined face, the
kindly eyes, and the familiar mane of unruly white hair, that
she could only stammer incoherently.

After a few moments, understanding dawned on Einstein's
face. "Ah! I think I understand. You're Emmy's mother, aren't
you?"

"Yes," she said, sighing in embarrassment, "and I'm so
sorry she's been coming over here and bothering you—"

"Bothering me! *Ach*, no!" he laughed. "Why, when a child
finds such joy in learning, then it is *my* joy to help her learn!
Please don't stop Emmy from coming to me with her school
problems. She is welcome in this house anytime."

And so it is between ourselves and God. Our problems loom
ominously over us—yet they are little more than a child's
school problems to the mind of the One who made the universe. We have a God who seeks fellowship with us, who
delights in talking with us, who points us to the solution to
our problems, and who sends us on our way encouraged and
emboldened to face our challenges.

When a need or hurt surfaces in your life, what is your first
response? Do you immediately go to God the Father in prayer?
If you're like me, prayer is often more of a last resort than a
first response. We go to prayer only after we have frantically
tried—and failed—to solve our problems in our own limited
strength.

James 5:13-16 directs the person who is in trouble to pray, and promises that his sin will be forgiven. The section concludes: "Therefore confess your sins to each other and pray for each other so that you may be healed. The prayer of a righteous man is powerful and effective." James is telling us something very important about prayer. Healing—emotional, spiritual, relational, and physical therapy—takes place when we prayerfully share our failures, our needs, and our sins with one another. This doesn't mean we need to dump every wrong thought and action before the entire congregation. Rather, the original Greek words in this passage suggest that there should be a context of protective intimacy as we confess to one another, such as is found in a small group or with one or two trusted friends.

When James goes on to say, "The prayer of a righteous man is powerful and effective," he uses a very interesting Greek word, *energeo*, to describe the quality of prayer he is talking about. It's the word from which we get our English word "energy." *Energeo* suggests that there is something dynamic and electrifying about this kind of prayer. Many of us would admit that there is very little dynamism or electricity in our prayers. How can we experience that kind of dynamic, effective prayer life? How can we learn to pray with *energeia*?

I don't believe God ever intended prayer to be a mystery or a secret. He wants all of us to have ready access to him in times of trouble, and to have fellowship with him at all times. So here are some guidelines which may help you begin to pray with *energeia*

First, become a student of the Bible. Throughout history, all the great men and women of prayer have been people who loved the Word of God. They were people who understood that it is impossible to pray effectively without a grasp of what God tells us about prayer in the Bible. Today, however, many of us seem content to be blissfully ignorant concerning the Bible's message about prayer. We have our pet biases, such as believing that God always says "yes" to our demands if we summon up enough faith, or believing that a certain prayer-formula can make us healthy and rich. But our biases about prayer don't always stand up to the truth of Scripture. Only when we understand prayer by studying the textbook of prayer, the Bible, can we truly begin to pray effectively and dynamically.

Second, beware of ritualism and repetition in your prayer life. Prayer does not need to be eloquent, standardized, memorized, or formal. God is sovereign and holy—but he is also our Father. That is why Paul said that we can approach God in prayer saying, "*Abba*, Father" (Romans 8:15; Galatians 4:6). *Abba* is the Aramaic equivalent to "Daddy," a term of familiarity and endearment. If you are a parent, you don't expect your children to approach you with flowery speeches, addressing you as "thee" and "thou" while speaking in Elizabethan English. Rather, you want your child to feel free to crawl into your lap and call you "Mommy" or "Daddy." And that's the kind of relationship God, your loving Father, desires with you.

I had a seminary professor who taught that public prayer should always be written out, never spontaneous. All grammar and sentence structure should be absolutely correct. If you weren't able to compose a written prayer, then you should read a prayer out of *The Book of Common Worship.* Yet I have a strong hunch that God doesn't care as much about mangled syntax, split infinitives, and dangling participles as he does about the human heart. God desires our love, not our ritual.

I wonder what we teach our children about prayer when we perpetuate ritual and repetition instead of biblical prayer. Many parents have used those familiar rhyming prayers to introduce their children to the practice of talking with God: "God is great, God is good; now we thank him for our food." Or, "Now I lay me down to sleep. I pray the Lord my soul to keep." Perhaps we do no great harm to our children by teaching them these rhymes. But I would suggest that neither do we do them a great service. Could it be that such rhymes actually convey the idea that prayer is a boring, repetitive exercise fit only for mealtimes and bedtime? Could it be that we are actually robbing our children of the vitality and spontaneity of the greatest experience in life— talking with God?

Prayer is an act of intimacy. Learning to pray is a process of becoming intimate with the Infinite in a natural way. As a student of prayer, I am learning to have the same kind of warm, ongoing, relaxed relationship with God that I enjoy with the members of my family. For example, one day my son Nathan came home after a playground fight with a friend. I said, "Nate, let's talk to God about that." Together we prayed for that boy and for Nathan's attitude. And then we watched God answer that prayer and heal their friendship. It was a great learning experience for Nathan—and for me—about prayer.

Third, beware of pride in prayer. Rituals, formulas, and formalities in prayer have a tendency to produce the sin of pride in us. The Pharisees in the Gospels prayed long, repetitive, proud prayers. "But when you pray," Jesus told his disciples in Matthew 6:5-6, "do not be like the hypocrites, for they love to pray standing in the synagogues and on the street corners to be seen by men. I tell you the truth, they have received their reward in full. When you pray, go into your room, close the door and pray to your Father, who is unseen. Then your Father, who sees what is done in secret, will reward you."

The proud, formal Pharisees disdained and judged those who could not pray as elegantly and properly as they. We often have the same problem with prayer today. We have our own prayer formulas and rituals. We insist that everyone must use 16 adjectives to address God before stating his name ("O most holy, gracious, sovereign, merciful . . ."). Or we require that the elements of prayer be in correct order:

first praise, then thanksgiving, then confession, then sup-
plication, then petition. And the people who don't pray the
way we pray are criticized or judged. That's the sin of pride.

X   I have been guilty of encouraging the sin of pride in others.
Many times in worship services I have complimented a fellow
pastor, a layman, or a seminary student who led in prayer by
saying, "That was a beautiful prayer"—as if what mattered
to God was a string of lofty words and elegant phrases. But
God isn't looking for impressive words. He wants an obedient
heart, not a lot of verbiage. And what he wants least of all is
our pride.

Fourth, pray continually—the very words of 1 Thessalo-
nians 5:17. Obviously, this doesn't mean we are to be on our
knees 24 hours a day. Rather, we are to be ready to talk to God
whenever and wherever the need or the opportunity arises.
Our prayer life is not to be a series of business appointments,
but a steady, ongoing relationship with our loving Father. A
vital prayer life involves an awareness of the continual presence of God with us. God doesn't keep office hours. He's
always available to us. So let us always be available to him in
prayer.

Regularly scheduled times of prayer are important because they prepare us to seek God at those unexpected times
when prayer for special wisdom, strength, or intervention
from God is urgently needed. Our family prays together at
breakfast, and my wife and I pray with each of our children at
bedtime. I also have my own private times of Bible study and
prayer. But equally important are those unscheduled prayer
times in the day when concerns arise and we immediately
seek God's solution.

Fifth, never make prayer a substitute for responsible action.
There are certain things that God can't do *for* us. He can only
do those things *with* us as we work in partnership with him.
If we pray for healing in a broken relationship, we also need
to take courageous steps toward reconciliation and forgiveness. If we pray to be forgiven by God, we must actively

choose to forgive ourselves. If we pray for a new beinning in life, we must actively let go of the past and embrace the future. In short, what we pray *for*, we must give ourselves *to*.

Sixth, be open to the unexpected ways God may answer your prayers. Ephesians 3:20 tells us that God "is able to do immeasurably more than all we ask or imagine, according to his power that is at work within us." I'm reminded of the little girl who asked her father for a nickel. Unable to find any change in his pocket, he reached into his wallet and handed his daughter a dollar bill. The little girl, never having handled paper money before, threw the dollar to the floor and began to cry. "I said I want a *nickel!*" she demanded. Sadly, this is the way we often react when God answers our prayers. As Ephesians 3:20 promises, God gives us more than we are able to ask or imagine—but it isn't always the answer we expect of him. Understanding that God is sovereign, gracious, and loving is an important step toward a dynamic, effective life of prayer.

We all need a little help sometimes distinguishing our areas of strength in prayer from our areas of neglect and need. I use five questions to help me evaluate the status of my prayer life. Perhaps these questions will be of similar help to you.

First, are you satisfied with your prayer life? This is a question you can only answer within your own heart.

Second, do you pray with confidence? Once you have offered your problem to the Lord in prayer, can you leave it there? Do you believe that your problem is now in God's hands and that he will act? Confidence in prayer grows primarily from two sources: time spent in the Bible and time spent in the experience of prayer itself. As we apply our Bible knowledge of prayer in the laboratory of life, we learn that God is a good listener, a reliable Friend, and a loving Father who responds to our prayers by giving us the good gifts of his infinite grace. As with any worthwhile endeavor in life, we gain confidence in prayer by *doing*.

Third, when someone comes to you with a problem and says, "Please pray for me," do you honor that request by praying specifically for that need? Or do you often fail to follow through on that promise? I find I'm more effective in my prayer for others when I make a commitment to keep in touch to see how they are progressing with the problem they shared with me. I write prayer requests in a pocket planner that I carry with me wherever I go. I check that planner daily, looking over the requests I have marked down in recent days and weeks. You could do the same with a wall calendar, a prayer notebook, a "things to do" list, or anything you consult regularly to help you organize your life.

Make a commitment to keep in touch with the person you are praying for. Ask specifically about his or her progress in overcoming the problem you're praying about. In doing so, you will bring greater discipline and consistency to your prayer life. You will also demonstrate genuine caring for that person and become an effective encourager to that person.

Fourth, are you consistently praying for at least five specific concerns? Five may not sound like a great number of prayer concerns. Yet as I talk to people about their personal prayer life, I find again and again that this is a very convicting question.

Fifth, do you balance your time in Bible study with time spent in meditation and prayer? And when you pray, do you spend all your time talking or do you also spend time listening?

We are children of a loving Father who seeks communion and intimate fellowship with us. When my children were very little, they didn't call me "Father" or even "Daddy." I was "Da-Da," a word that sounds like "Abba," Paul's term picturing our relationship to our heavenly Father. One of my warmest memories is the picture of my little children almost asleep in their beds. With their eyes half-closed, they would murmur, " 'Night, Da-Da. I love you, Da-Da."

I suspect there is a similar fondness in the heart of our heavenly Father as we approach him in childlike humility and faith. In Matthew 19:14 Jesus said, "Let the little children come to me, and do not hinder them, for the kingdom of heaven belongs to such as these." Indeed, the most profound message about prayer in the Scriptures is that we can go to the Creator of the invisible atoms and the farthest galaxies and call him "Daddy." We don't need to grovel before him, burn sacrifices, or slash our bodies. We can simply approach him like children. As our loving Father, he will smile upon us with fatherly pride, lift us up, and gently invite us to whisper in his ear.

There is no thought, no feeling, no hurt that we cannot bring to him. Even when we feel like crying out to God, as Jesus did on the cross, "Why have you forsaken me?," he will accept our questions. We can bring all our deepest feelings to God because he is our Abba, our Father—our "Da-Da."

While writing this book, I have watched a family go to their heavenly Daddy with their honest feelings. My friends David and Edie Bizot have been in continual contact with the Infinite as they have loved their eight-year-old son through his battle with terminal cancer.

I received a call from Edie at about one thirty one morning. "I don't think Kevin will be with us much longer," she said. Her voice, though controlled, was eloquent with emotion and exhaustion. "He didn't come through the surgery too well, Ron, and he's in a coma. They've put him on a respirator and he's barely breathing. Could you come?"

I drove to Kaiser Hospital in Redwood City and spent the rest of the night and most of the next day with David and Edie. I watched this father and mother minister to their little boy during the last hours of his life. I thought about how special and happy little Kevin was, and how much this little boy—like his father and mother—loved Jesus.

The nurses gently placed Kevin in his father's arms, despite the monitors and IV tubes that were attached to him. David rocked Kevin for a long time as I talked with Edie. "Kevin was just on loan to us, Ron," she said softly. "For however long we have them, our children are just on loan to us. We care for them and love them. And when the time comes, we give them back to our heavenly Father. We know that Kevin really belongs to God."

We prayed together for awhile. Then it was Edie's turn to hold Kevin. She rocked him, stroked his face, and whispered to him. David said to me, "Edie and I don't want Kevin to be snatched from us. We want to offer him back to God." So we placed our hands on this precious little boy and gave him back to God. We thanked God for Kevin's eight beautiful years of life.

A short time later, little Kevin left his parents' arms and was lifted into the arms of his loving Father.

My hospital vigil with David and Edie reminded me of the difference between how Christians and nonChristians face life and death—a difference made by a vital prayer life, a vital love-relationship with God. Throughout Kevin's illness, David and Edie took all their feelings—anger, doubts, questions, pain—to their heavenly Daddy. They knew they were loved, accepted, and embraced by the grace of the One who was not only their God, but their Friend, Father, and "Da-Da."

Prayer is the open line of communication between you and the God of a new beginning. As you set out on your quest for God's new beginning in your life, your greatest delight will come from journeying deeper and deeper into the heart of God. The discipline of daily devotion to God in prayer is a discipline of relationship, revelation, and joy. God lovingly invites us into intimate fellowship with him—a dynamic intimacy charged with the life-changing *energeia* of prayer.

18

The Key

The grace of God struck like a bolt from heaven on a Friday afternoon more than a dozen years ago.

My friend Tim was a sophomore in college. After his last class of the week, he jumped behind the wheel of his Toyota pickup and started for home. It was about a 40-mile commute between the campus and his parents' hilltop ranch house east of town. Tim rolled down the window and turned on the radio. The fragrance from the fields and orchards breezed through the cab of his truck as the speedometer climbed to 50.

At the same moment in another city, Tim's grandmother Anna was serving coffee to a weekly prayer group that met in her home. Her prayer partners were an eclectic group—a Mennonite, a Nazarene, two Pentecostals, a Baptist, and a Catholic.

After coffee they sang a hymn and began to pray together. Suddenly one of the men in the group looked up at the hostess. "Anna, do you have a grandson who lives in the mountains?" he asked.

"Yes!" she answered. "Why do you ask?"

"I think we should pray for him," the man replied. "I believe he is in danger just now." So the group prayed together for Tim.

As they were praying, Tim was steering his pickup around a curve toward a narrow bridge spanning a dry riverbed. A car approached the bridge from the other side, dead-center in the road, straddling the double yellow line. Tim wasn't unduly alarmed at the sight. Drivers who carelessly cut corners were a common hazard on these winding mountain roads. Tim sounded his horn and said aloud, "Hey, buddy, move over!"

But after crossing the bridge the onrushing car remained in the middle of the road. Horrified, Tim realized that the driver had no intention of assuming his own lane. Tim cranked the wheel and hit the brakes simultaneously. His pickup skidded into the thick dust of the shoulder just as the car whistled past, missing a violent collision by less than a foot. The pickup fish-tailed and finally came to rest in a cloud of dust as the car roared around the curve and disappeared. Just a few feet to Tim's right was a steep embankment which dropped into the riverbed. Just a few feet from the front bumper was the concrete bridge abutment.

Shortly after Tim arrived home, the phone rang in the ranch house on the hill. Tim's mother answered.

"Is Tim all right?" Anna asked with concern in her voice.

"He just walked in a few minutes ago and he was as white as a sheet!" Tim's mother answered. "He was run off the road by a wild driver. He said it was a miracle he wasn't killed. But how did you know he was in danger?"

You can imagine the joy and amazement of this family as the story unfolded.

Sometimes the grace of God is like that: invading our lives in ways that are sudden, inexplicable, and awe-inspiring, commanding our attention in a miraculous way. Yet God's grace surrounds us continuously like the air we breathe. And just as we live most of our days without thinking about the air that gives us life, so we tend to live largely unaware of the all-suffusing grace of God.

I believe it is possible to learn to see and feel God's pervasive grace in our lives. As we become increasingly attuned to the ways his grace touches us every moment, we will sense the continual reality of his presence. We will feel our hand in his as he leads us and draws us closer to himself.

Grace becomes very real to us when we experience the miraculous, as my friend Tim experienced in his close brush with death. But grace is just as real when it comes to us in the pleasure of a sunny, relaxing day, the delight of a good book, or the comfort of a visit with close friends. His grace is just as real when we find it in a new and unexpected insight from Scripture or in the strength God gives us to endure an illness, a hardship, or an act of unjust treatment.

If we fail to realize that these events are the result of God being with us, then we will unwittingly ascribe the benefits of his grace to fate, luck, or coincidence. But when our eyes are open to truly see the grace of God, our day-to-day existence is transformed into a thrilling adventure of discovery. We no longer drift through life toward some uncertain destiny. Rather, we have a sense of direction and progress in life. We know that our lives have meaning. Even our pain has a purpose: to make us more like Christ.

For many people, the journey toward a new beginning and a greater identification with Christ seems to be a lonely journey. Yet this pilgrimage need not—in fact, it *cannot*—be undertaken alone. The Christian life must be lived out in community as we mutually build, encourage, and uphold one another along the way. If you are feeling alone in your search for a new beginning, could it be that you have actually *chosen* the loneliness of your solitary journey?

In his book, *Stretcher Bearers*, Michael Slater describes an incident which illustrates how some of us irrationally prefer stoic self-reliance over life itself. Slater was bodysurfing at a California beach when he saw a 13-year-old boy floundering

in the surf about 75 feet away. Slater knew immediately that
something was wrong. He swam to the boy, took him under
one arm, and brought him back to the beach.

After catching his breath, Slater said to the boy, "You were
drowning out there, weren't you?"

"Yes," the boy answered, dropping his eyes.

"Why didn't you cry out for help?" Slater asked.

The boy looked up sharply. "What would my friends think
if I cried out for help?"[1]

How incredibly foolish this young man was! He would have
died before he cried out for help! But are we so different from
this young man? At some point in our lives each of us has
floundered helplessly under the weight of grief, guilt, stress,
depression, doubt, or fear. But did we cry out for help?

"What would my friends think if I cried out for help?"

I've heard all the reasons people give for trying to solve
their problems alone: "My folks raised me to stand on my own
two feet;" "I don't want to be a burden to anyone;" "Nobody
would like me if they knew me as I really am;" "Nobody else
could really understand what I'm going through;" "I don't
take charity;" "I don't need anybody's pity." Excuses! Proud,
foolish excuses!

Because I'm a pastor, counselor, and author, people often
look to me as a person with the answers. But I have hurts,
fears, guilt feelings, inadequacies, and failures too—and I
look to *others* for the answers. Many times in the last few
years I felt like I was drowning and I cried out for help.
Sometimes I had to overcome the temptation to offer those
same proud, foolish excuses—but I know my own weakness.
So I went to others for advice, encouragement, and prayer—
and I asked them to hold me accountable in my areas of
weakness.

Grant Teaff, head coach of the Baylor University football
team, made this statement a few years ago, explaining why
he had given his life to Jesus Christ: "I'm not particularly
religious. It's just that I've learned that I'm weak and I need

help." You don't usually hear statements like that from brawny, "go get 'em" guys like coaches. But Grant Teaff had the courage and sense to admit what is true for us all: we're weak and we need help. It's been said that if the self-made man had it to do all over again, he'd ask for help. It's true. If you've been afraid to cry out for help, it's time to admit the truth about yourself: you're weak and you need the help of God and other Christians.

I need the encouragement and support of my family. So I seek to be honest and authentic before my loved ones, sharing not only my joys but my sorrows and stresses as well. I need to be accountable for my life-style. So I have close Christian friends to whom I voluntarily submit myself, asking them to watch my life, question me, and check on my progress toward my goals as a follower of Jesus Christ. Sometimes I need specialized help that my family and friends can't provide. So there have been times when I have consulted professional Christian counselors for insight into my problems.

You may be at a point where you know you need help, perhaps even specialized professional help. What's holding you back? Is it pride? Are you afraid of what someone else will think of you? Would you really rather drown in your problem than cry out for help? That's what is happening to you. You are drowning under the weight of your problems. You are dying a little each day. This is so important to understand: Reaching out to others and seeking the help you need is a sign of strength and courage, not weakness.

God is with us and all around us in the grand miracles and small pleasures that enter our lives. But he also comes to us through people. He has given us family members and Christian friends who care for us and lovingly support us. He has provided gifted pastoral and professional counselors to bring insight, understanding, and healing to us in our times of hurt and confusion.

God's presence surrounds us and sustains us as we meet him in prayer and in the pages of his Word. It is in God alone, as Paul said in Acts 17:28, that "we live and move and have our being." And it is ultimately God alone who must be the focus and object of our desire. It is in him alone that we must find our joy, worth, and contentment.

There is a minister named John Linn who travels throughout Scandinavia with a unique approach to ministry. He goes to a church in the community and ministers first to the children in the church. After spending a week teaching and encouraging the children, Linn concludes the week with a special worship service led by the children.

At one service in a little Swedish village, Linn asked if any of the children would like to recite Psalm 23:1. One little girl, only four-and-a-half years old, raised her hand and shyly came forward. She began, "The Lord is my shepherd. He's all I want." Then she sat down.

I believe that little girl said it all. Though she misquoted the psalm, she demonstrated a profound insight into its truth: "The Lord is my shepherd. He's all I want."

But is he? Is God really all we want? Or would we have to confess that we are seeking joy in other things—in financial security, a career, or plans for a leisure-filled retirement? Perhaps you are seeking your joy in building a reputation for yourself or in building a business. Perhaps you are seeking joy by acquiring the symbols of success—a bigger home, a newer car, a sailboat, a hideaway in the mountains. You may even be seeking your fulfillment in church activities, winning approval for all the wonderful things you are accomplishing on the church board, in the Sunday school, or in the choir. Sometimes our desire for what is merely *good* can blind us to what is truly *best*.

"The Lord is my shepherd. He's all I want." We will never be happy until God himself is the object of all our affections.

The early years of the 19th century were troubled times in the German confederation. Rumors of revolution and rioting had the federated government in panic. Klemens von Metternich, the chief statesman of the confederation, ordered thousands of young men drafted into the army to guard the borders and put down internal revolts. Across the countryside, young men in uniform tramped off to an unknown destiny.

In one German village stood a grand old stone-walled church with an ornately carved facade, beautiful stained glass, and a stately pipe-organ. The organ was famed throughout the region for its beautiful, rich tone. One day the aged caretaker of the church was interrupted during his chores by a knock on the great oak door of the sanctuary. He opened the door to find a young man in uniform on the steps.

"Sir, I have a favor to ask," the young soldier began. "Would you please permit me to play the organ for one hour?"

"I'm sorry, young man," the caretaker replied. "No one but our own organist is permitted to play the organ."

"But sir, I've heard so much about the organ of this church, and I've walked so many miles just to see it, just to play it for a single hour!"

The aged man paused, then shook his head sadly.

"Please," the soldier pleaded. "My commander gave me a 24-hour leave. In a few more days we move to another province where the fighting is expected to be heavy. This may be the last chance in my life to play the organ."

The caretaker reluctantly nodded. He swung the door open and beckoned the soldier inside. Then he took a key from his pocket and held it out to the soldier. "The organ is locked," he said. "Here is the key."

The soldier took the key and unlocked the ornate cabinet of the organ. Then he began to play. A billow of majestic chords rolled from the great golden pipes of the organ. The caretaker stood transfixed as the glorious music washed over him, bringing tears to his eyes. He moved to one of the pews and sat down, as if entranced.

Within minutes, people from the village gathered at the church doorway and peered in. Removing their hats, the villagers stepped into the sanctuary and sat down to listen.

Streams of beautiful music filled the sanctuary for one hour. Then the gifted fingers of the organist struck a final chord and lifted from the keyboard.

The young man closed and locked the keyboard cabinet. As he stood and turned, he was surprised to see that the church had nearly filled with parishioners who had laid aside their chores to listen to his music. Humbly receiving their compliments, the young soldier walked down the center aisle to return the key to the caretaker. "Thank you," the young man whispered.

The old man rose to his feet and took the key. "Thank *you*," he answered, grasping the young soldier's gifted hands. "Young man, that was the most beautiful music these old ears have ever heard. What is your name?"

"My name is Felix," replied the soldier. "Felix Mendelssohn."

The old caretaker's eyes widened as he realized whose hands he grasped—the hands of the young man who, before he was 20 years old, had become one of the most celebrated composers on the European continent. The old man's gaze followed the young soldier as he left the church and disappeared into the village street.

"To think," the old man wondered aloud, "the master was here and I almost failed to give him the key!"

So it is with us. The Master is here. God is with us. His grace envelops us. If you give him the key to your heart, he can make unimaginably beautiful music in your life—music that will make the world stop, listen, and wonder. The Master is here and he is ready to transform us by his grace. He is ready to give us a new beginning. It is not only our duty but our joy to give him the key to all that we are and have.

Notes

Chapter Six—Dead End or New Beginning?
1. Keith Miller, *Sin: Overcoming the Ultimate Deadly Addiction* (Harper and Row, Publishers), pp. 172, 175-176.

Chapter Seven—The Hands of a Servant
1. Linda (Marchiano) Lovelace with Mike McGrady, *Out of Bondage* (Lyle Stuart Inc., 1986), p. 198.

Chapter Eight—How Well Do You Know Your Father?
1. George Orick, "A Second Chance," *Reader's Digest* (November 1983), p. 85.

Chapter Nine—The Threshold of a New Life
1. Dietrich Bonhoeffer, *The Cost of Discipleship* (The Macmillan Company, 1963, second edition), pp. 45-48, italics in the original.

Chapter Ten—The Fire Alarm
1. From "Giving In," an anonymous first-person account in the book by Philip Yancey and Tim Stafford, *Unhappy Secrets of the Christian Life* (Zondervan, 1979), pp. 56-59.

Chapter Eleven—The Truth About Consequences
1. "In a Little While," from the album *Age to Age*, copyright © 1982 by Word, Inc. Words and music by Amy Grant and Michael W. Smith. Used by permission.

Chapter Twelve—Dream a New Dream
1. Quotes from Jamie Buckingham's *Where Eagles Soar* reprinted in Dean Merrill's *Another Chance: How God Overrides Our Big Mistakes* (Zondervan, 1981), p. 192.
2. J.I. Packer, *Knowing God* (InterVarsity Press, 1973), p. 219.
3. M. Scott Peck, *The Road Less Traveled* (Touchstone/Simon and Schuster, 1978), p. 15.
4. John Claypool, *The Light Within You* (Word Books, 1983), p. 192.

Chapter Thirteen—Alone Again
1. Jim Smoke, *Living Beyond Divorce* (Harvest House, 1984), pp. 60-61.
2. Ibid., p. 35.

Chapter Fourteen—The Deep Places of the Soul
1. Herbert Freudenberger, *Burn-Out* (Bantam Books, 1980), p. 17.
2. H. Norman Wright, *Now I Know Why I'm Depressed (And What I Can Do About It)* (Harvest House, 1984), pp. 71-72.

Chapter Fifteen—Prone to Wander
1. C.S. Lewis, *The Screwtape Letters* (Macmillan Co., 1943), p. 65.
2. *Discipleship Journal*, Sept. 1987, Cal Thomas (interview), "Moral Failures and Small Groups," p. 42.

Chapter Sixteen—Deliver Us from Evil
1. Dietrich Bonhoeffer, *Creation and Fall/Temptation* (Macmillan Co., 1959), pp. 116-117.
2. Miller, *Sin: Overcoming the Ultimate Deadly Addiction*, p. 65.
3. Ibid., p. 66.
4. *Time*, Sept. 28, 1987, Dan Goodgame, "I Do Believe in Control," p. 64.

Chapter Eighteen—The Key
1. Michael Slater, *Stretcher Bearers* (Regal Books, 1985), pp. 51-52.

Other Good
Harvest House Reading

THE CHURCH IS NOT FOR PERFECT PEOPLE
by *William J. Murray*

New Christians versus lifelong Christians—Can the struggles of relating to each other be overcome in the church? William J. Murray, son of Madalyn Murray O'Hair and author of the bestseller *My Life Without God*, reveals the kinds of problems he and many new Christians face as they try to fit into the modern church. *The Church Is Not for Perfect People* covers topics such as learning the language and clichés of the Christian church; facing marital discord when one spouse does not receive Christ; the struggle of singles—especially divorced singles—who try to fit into a church geared to couples; and the lack of church support for new Christians who need help dealing with past problems such as alcohol, drug abuse, and sexual temptations. *The Church Is Not for Perfect People* takes a much-needed and realistic look at how the church can be supportive of Christians who are emerging from a humanistic society.

BLOW AWAY THE BLACK CLOUDS
by *Florence Littauer*

Sympathetically, Florence helps the reader to come to terms with the emotional handicap of depression, offers practical insight on how to determine the cause—physical, psychological, or spiritual—and maps out the guidelines for constructive action to overcome depression.

BOUNCING BACK
by *William Coleman*

Rejection is coming, just like bad weather! How we cope with its devastating effects will mean the difference between success and failure in our lives. Bestselling author William Coleman's compassionate approach and godly counsel will help you turn the hurt of rejection into building blocks for a healthy self-image.

GROWING THROUGH DIVORCE
by *Jim Smoke*

Here is a practical guide for anyone facing divorce. This book can transform your life from an old ending to a new beginning and help to heal the deep hurts and doubts of anyone trapped in the despair of divorce. Includes a working guide to help you discover for yourself how to deal with the pain of the moment and develop new goals for tomorrow.

OVERCOMING HURTS AND ANGER
by *Dr. Dwight Carlson*

Dr. Carlson shows us how to confront our feelings and negative emotions in order to experience liberation and fulfillment. He presents seven practical steps to help us identify and cope with our feelings of hurt and anger.

Dear Reader:

We would appreciate hearing from you regarding this Harvest House nonfiction book. It will enable us to continue to give you the best in Christian publishing.

1. What most influenced you to purchase *Courage to Begin Again*?
   ☐ Author
   ☐ Subject matter
   ☐ Backcover copy
   ☐ Recommendations
   ☐ Cover/Title
   ☐ _____

2. Where did you purchase this book?
   ☐ Christian bookstore
   ☐ General bookstore
   ☐ Other
   ☐ Grocery store
   ☐ Department store

3. Your overall rating of this book:
   ☐ Excellent ☐ Very good ☐ Good ☐ Fair ☐ Poor

4. How likely would you be to purchase other books by this author?
   ☐ Very likely
   ☐ Somewhat likely
   ☐ Not very likely
   ☐ Not at all

5. What types of books most interest you?
   (check all that apply)
   ☐ Women's Books
   ☐ Marriage Books
   ☐ Current Issues
   ☐ Self Help/Psychology
   ☐ Bible Studies
   ☐ Fiction
   ☐ Biographies
   ☐ Children's Books
   ☐ Youth Books
   ☐ Other _____

6. Please check the box next to your age group.
   ☐ Under 18   ☐ 25-34   ☐ 45-54
   ☐ 18-24   ☐ 35-44   ☐ 55 and over

Mail to: Editorial Director
Harvest House Publishers
1075 Arrowsmith
Eugene, OR 97402

Name _____

Address _____

City _____ State _____ Zip _____

Thank you for helping us to help you in future publications!